Six MONTHS to LIVE

MAKING EACH DAY MATTER

CATHY ANELLO

BALBOA PRESS

A DIVISION OF HAY HOUSE

Balboa Press books may be ordered through booksellers or by contacting:

Balboa Press
A Division of Hay House
1663 Liberty Drive
Bloomington, IN 47403
www.balboapress.com
1 (877) 407-4847

Print information available on the last page.

ISBN: 978-1-5043-5427-1 (sc)
ISBN: 978-1-5043-5428-8 (e)

Library of Congress Control Number: 2016904856

Balboa Press rev. date: 05/24/2016

CONTENTS

Who I Am xiii

Month 1 1
    Week 1: Tolerance 3
    Week 2: Getting Real In My Relationships 8
    Week 3: The Joy Jumps 14
    Week 4: De-Stress Yourself 20

Month 2 29
    Week 5: Change..31
    Week 6: The R-Word 36
    Week 7: The Path To Health 46
    Week 8: The Truth (Live Your Authentic Self) 54

Month 3 63
    Week 9: The Drama Detachment.................................65
    Week 10: Today 72
    Week 11: One Day In America....................................76
    Week 12: Every Encounter Matters 86

Month 4 91
    Week 13: Gratitude Attitude 93
    Week 14: Don't Ignore The Signs...............................100
    Week 15: Our Children, Our Future 106
    Week 16: Hanging On Vs Letting Go 110

Month 5 117
    Week 17: Thank You For Being A Friend 119
    Week 18: They Say It's Your Birthday 128
    Week 19: Mi Famiglia 135
    Week 20: Choices = Consequences 141

Month 6 149
    Week 21: The Path To Self-Love 151
    Week 22: Forgiveness 158
    Week 23: What Is Death...Really? 166
    Week 24: Simple Truths Along The Way 175

Changes In Me: 183
Thank You! 187
About The Author 197

What if a doctor told you that you only had six months to live?

SIX MONTHS.
What would you do with your life?
How would you live it?
Would you go through each day as you did yesterday,
before you "knew" of this inevitable expiration date?
Or...
Would you be inspired to take off the rose-colored glasses
and start excavating deep layers inside yourself?
For the life you
Wished you had lived?
(The one you told yourself you would be living ten years down the road)
When the children are grown.
When I retire.
When I have enough money.
With this news, you begin to ask yourself,
How would I treat people?
How would I let people treat me?
How would I leave all those unsettled areas of my life?
What would matter now?
Who would matter now?
I know you are thinking – crazy thought.
Or...

Maybe, because we have no idea when or how we will be called to leave this human existence, we should be paying much closer attention to the things in life that really matter now. Paying attention to the things that excite us, ignite a light inside of us, and effortlessly lead the way towards our fulfillment. If each day was potentially our last day, it gives us only one more day to love; one more day to laugh; one more day to hug the people we love and connect with them.

I started this journey with a twitter post. Innocently, I woke up one day and posted on my twitter page, *"I don't know how I want to live, I only know #howImnotgoingtolive."*

Motivated by a stressed out, crazy, repetitious day, filled with berating directions from an abusive tyrant of a boss, this post forced me to look at who I had become, and ultimately led to a huge change in my life. A loud voice came out of nowhere and I heard these words: *"Cathy, would you be acting this way if you only had six months to live?"*

I got up from my desk filled with payroll reports, unimportant emails, request upon request I had to answer, and I closed my office door. Then I sat and stared at my twitter post for what seemed like an hour. I felt blank. Wallowing in a worn out 'day in the life' of Cathy, I wondered how my life would be different if I had been given this life verdict.

I was suddenly flooded with internal questions. Why was it okay with me that people walked all over me? Why was it that every day that I tried to bring positivity into an environment I was passionate about, I allowed the negativity and drama to cloud my true feelings? I allowed my desire for money to cloud out my integrity and my values concerning my innermost desire of living a happier life. In retrospect, I felt I was being shot down at every move. Even though I had made a movement towards a better way of working and living, I could please nobody, and as a result, I certainly wasn't the cheeriest butterfly in the garden.

The thought lingered every day, in every moment I allowed myself to be present. By allowing myself to be present, I was forced to look at things as they are, not how my mind could replay and spin them. One thing was certainly clear: my life was spiraling out of control.

The most organic change in me was the awareness that every single day in our life matters in some way for someone. Even when we're feeling unimportant, unloved, undesired, and engulfed in the darkness that may surround us, we still matter to someone. If we die today, we will matter to someone. That simple awareness ignited a desire to be clear who those "someone's" were.

I wondered constantly how we would live our lives if we knew when the end would come. I didn't know how this journey would end. I couldn't have dreamed of the ways in which it would transform me.

When we're able to stop for long enough and look at each day in life as the gift that it is: good, great, bad or ugly, we can simply take on the day in front of us. Through some extreme highs and lows, I was finally allowed to decide what was best for *my life*. There were moments when I stood there stunned at what I had experienced. Moments when my mouth dropped open in disbelief, while I discovered life and death on life's terms.

I could not have predicted the life experiences that would come my way after that one sentence or the power of retracing the moments in my life that serendipitously showed the path behind me. This writing experience showed me that without a doubt nothing is random. It cemented my belief that all living things are connected by pure energy, from humans to animals, plants, and sea creatures.

I became aware that every person or creature that has come into my life was there for a reason. We all have a beating heart. We all have lungs that give us breath every single moment to sustain life, and a shining soul spirit oozing with the desire to feel the joy of being alive through that body of energy. The feeling of true human-to-human connectedness is what allows our hearts to open, and thankfully to soften. It dissolves anger and eliminates fear. I hope this will be the greatest gift that you take away from this book.

It became very clear to me that all we have is now.

Dying and Death

Although, I knew this wasn't going to be a book about dying, it became a provocative question. What really happens when we die? Do we have a choice when we arrive on the other side? Is it simply our time to go, which means we can "live" without fear of this event?

Alternatively, is it a matter of random acts in the universe, and when we get to that moment we can choose whether to stay or go? Each time I came close to an answer, life steered me in another mystical direction. One tragic day when a close family member was killed in a head-on collision, I threw my hands in the air, looked up, and said, 'What the hell is happening here?"

When you are stunned with the death of someone you care about, the fear of your own death dissolves and you find yourself talking to their spirit as if they are still here. With death, when you get past the grief, you discover the connection you had with this person went far beyond their physical existence. Through this process, I broke this fear pattern and began to live my life as Dr. Wayne Dyer put it at a seminar I attended in Portland a few months ago...

"Fearlessly"

Sixteen years ago on March 5, 1999, my sixty-five-year-old Mother died after only knowing of the possibility for six weeks. The day she died, I watched her spirit lift to heaven. I literally observed her spirit rise in pure white energy. Her death was apparently on her terms, because every week of her life in my teenage years I heard her say, "Well, my Mother died at fifty-eight, so I'm lucky if I make it to sixty-five." Although witnessing my Mother's death was one of the most incredible confirmations of life after death, I often wondered how she would have lived her last bit of life if she'd been given six months' notice, rather than six weeks. She lived in fear every day of her life. She constantly worried about other people's lives, never stopping for a minute to wonder what it would be like to live her own life.

With what I know today, she may very well have pre-supposed her death by her thoughts and her words, and quite possibly she chose her exit date before she even entered this world. This particular question is one I would ask for many years to come.

My Grandmother was staunch in her conviction that she never wanted to die. Even at her sickest at the age of 105, she looked at me and said *"I'm not ready to go yet, honey."* When her time came, I witnessed her dance with the other side of life. Preparing herself to lose all fear and walk through the thin veil of life and death. Calling out her husbands name who had passed 55 years before, even blowing him kisses. Telling me not to bother her as she was about to "have lunch" with an Aunt and a sister who crossed over long ago. To me giving absolute proof that she was with her most precious loved ones when she left us. It was the most beautiful, inspiring display of strength and grace to witness. If you are lucky enough to reach this age, you will lose your filter. You will say what you want to say, and if you are capable, you will do what you want to do. I promise, you will no longer care what anybody thinks.

Shortly before she died the doctor looked at us and said, *'Well I hate to say this, but I don't think she's going to make it five more years."* We laughed. She laughed. Our last days with her had us singing, dancing, and talking about the past. Watching the full circle of life was such a gift to me. She stopped eating at the kitchen table, preferring to sit at her picture window and watch the world go by, but it always stuck with me that she got up and put on her makeup and her jewelry every single day.

I dedicate this book to my Mother's and
Grandmother's last six months.

WHO I AM

"I can only be me, whoever that is."

-Bob Dylan

Like all of us, I wear different hats at different times and I do a multitude of diverse tasks, from the insignificant to the important. We all have our labels. I'm a daughter, a sister, a mother, a girlfriend, a grandmother, a granddaughter, a loyal friend, and a fierce fighter for what I believe in, yet I'm emotional and vulnerable when I allow myself to feel hurt or I'm out of touch with my inner child. I'm a lover when love is reciprocal, and I've always been a runner. Not the cardio kind, but the unable to face it kind. I learned at a very early age the art of detachment, and I've recently realized the toxic side of this quality. When I'm done, I'm done. However, it was never a strong suit of mine to know when that time was.

I was born into a typical suburban family in the late fifties; a time when having children (lots of them) was the thing to do. Most families had a minimum of three to five children. We moved to Marin County in the early seventies where I quickly transformed from a sheltered city girl to a new way of living in suburbia. Little did I know growing up, that this was a persona.

My parents bought their home in a small cul-de-sac of Model Homes. These homes became the playground for the neighborhood kids. We played make believe that we were grown-ups, as if they were our own.

I grew up with four strong-willed macho Italian brothers. The only girl in a mass of testosterone. I was completely blinded to how that testosterone environment and all that goes with being a boy would both help and hinder me throughout my life. Because of that environment, I have a strong will and I'm feisty. I don't back down from a fight, and I stand up to anyone when I believe in my cause. This had always been either too intimidating for the men in my life or too masculine for the pretty girls who I wanted to befriend.

Even though I'm a tomboy at heart, I love my make-up, lashes and, high heels. I love Hollywood trendy, and I'm a big shades on kind of girl. There was a time when I was sixteen and decked out in jeans, a white t-shirt, and tattered leather coat that my Grandmother lectured me on the value of being a girl. Clearly, she was trying to manipulate me out of that attire to bring out the softer side of me. I never forgot that moment, but it would be years before softness became a part of me.

Over the years, heartbreak and becoming a grandmother at a young age changed me. I became a grandmother at the young age of thirty-six.

The fact that I wouldn't allow this beautiful child to call me Grandma (I'm still Cathy to her) clearly reminds me that I have also spent a great deal of my life being very vain. I've never been able to look at myself as perfect the way I am; either my face was too long, I had one wrinkle too many, too many grey hairs, muffin top (oh no) or I'm getting too old (oh no). The truth is I never had a relationship with my own physical body that was loving or self-caring, until now. I often tried to be many different people, and inevitably, in that process, I lost myself.

I've often wondered if I'd felt comfortable in my skin in my teen years, would I have held captive my strong sense of vanity? What if, during those important growing years, being me had been enough? What would that have felt like, instead of trying to be any and everyone else but me.

When you become aware that you're looking at the potential end of your life, you get really clear and take quick, spiritual and physical hold of your sacred self like there's no tomorrow. The vanity vanishes and you crave the real healthy authentic self. You crave a daily life in alignment with who you really are.

Perhaps by living everybody's life, I never took the opportunity to just be "me."

This will be important to me in the days to come. With six months to live, do I pay more attention to others or to myself?

I'm about to find out.

"Almost everything – all external expectations, all pride, all fear of embarrassment or failure – these things just fall away in the face of death, leaving only what is truly important. Remembering that you are going to die is the best way I know to avoid the trap of thinking you have something to lose. You are already naked. There is no reason not to follow your heart."

- Steve Jobs (1955—2011)

MONTH 1

WEEK 1: TOLERANCE

Nobody can hurt me without my permission."

-*MAHATAMI GHANDI*

I've learned in rather rapid sequence that tolerance is a quality I have a bit too much of. I'm clear that life is about lessons, so I'll always take the lessons.

According to the dictionary, to tolerate is to; bear, abide, endure, put up with, stand for. ★

With the six months to live theory I recognize that for far too long I've gone through life pushing important things under the rug for the sake of "saving face" or to keep the peace, or maybe even to convince myself that I didn't need to be right all of the time. I often tiptoed around my life pulling the eggshells out of my feet.

It always seemed that if I endured, I was strong. If I forged on with my eyes closed, poof, it went away. In other words, I usually buried it. Tolerance became a mask for avoidance.

I've learned that the human spirit that has 'endured" has a distinct breaking point of no return. When we bury our true feelings about anything, they can lay dormant for a long time. While it becomes a great defense mechanism to go on with our lives in spite of the event, historic events in our lives tells us that nothing stays buried forever. You'll eventually have to look at yourself or the situation you're avoiding.

Perhaps in this particular situation I had endured more than most should. Putting responsibility or even love for others first, before you

3

or your own feelings, often comes with a price tag. Unconditional love and understanding, and unconditional forgiveness, with all its bells and whistles, actually take on some form of tolerance. Thank God for tolerance, however when we tolerate past the level of our capacity, the situation we're "tolerating" does funny things to our psyche. It lingers and clings to us until we take action to shed or walk away from them; this is no easy task. There are times when defending a position requires too much emotional energy, so instead we tolerate it.

When we step into a mode of tolerance, we end up with feelings of self-betrayal. As we allow people to hurt us or we try to fix someone else, justify someone's behavior, or even pretend something does not exist, it stays hidden deep inside of us, silently weighing us down like a bag of concrete. This heavyhearted feeling usually symbolizes that this situation isn't over. We have simply shelved it.

While reading *A Course in Miracles*, the line, *"In my defenselessness, my safety lies"* spoke to me in a distinct way. I became clear that I had to stop positioning myself in a way that constantly required me to tell people who or what I'm really all about. I became acutely aware that I always explain myself or my actions to other people; why I did this, or why I did that, and then, like a light bulb received the insight as to what a waste of time that is.

Why was I explaining my position, my thoughts, or what I felt was right to a person who felt their way was right? It now made much more sense to me to own my truth, let other people own theirs, and explain my actions only when asked. Anything short of that was a waste of my time and energy. There's no reason to apologize or provide explanations for being who you are. Once you stop giving justification, you become who you truly are and start living your life in wondrous ways.

As I dig into this emotion called tolerance, I'm trying to understand its purpose in my life. With six months to live my life, exactly how tolerant do I want or need to be?

Why do we tolerate things we absolutely know don't serve us? I find myself cringing at the word itself, yet I'm also clear that I do it a lot.

Around the world every day, there are documented events of human beings forced into situations who tolerate the unthinkable. There are high-income athletes being bullied every week in a locker room. They keep quiet in order to play the sport they love and collect their paycheck. There are wives, in many public and private arenas, who have tolerated years of physical and emotional abuse in order to continue living an extravagant lifestyle.

There are presidents, leaders, and celebrities who tolerate the press constantly discrediting them. They can't even go to a store and purchase a drink without it being grandstanded into some hidden agenda.

According to the AFCARS REPORT from the U.S. Department of Health and Human Services there are more than 400,000 children placed into foster homes in the United States with families they don't know. These children have to learn tolerance in their new surroundings simply to survive.

There are many situations in our lives, from simple daily life to the extreme, where tolerance is an absolute. It's the necessary emotion to get us through tough situations with grace. There's a place for tolerance, simply to avoid feeling uncomfortable or to avoid becoming upset. Therefore, in some situations, tolerance is necessary to survive.

However, in order to live your best life, your tolerance levels should become very selective.

It is true that, "The only way out is through." This line has influenced me throughout my entire life. When you're tolerating something that isn't serving you, something that's bringing you down instead of lifting you up, you aren't living, you are simply enduring.

So what if, instead of tolerating, you spoke up?

Clearly, the foster children and the bullied have important reasons to tolerate, as that is simple survival. However, while sometimes necessary, tolerance blocks who you really are. On a journey of self-discovery and living as if each day mattered, it was important to me to identify exactly what was intolerable to me.

Perhaps you pride yourself as being a "tolerant" person and can internally justify the need to tolerate, but you need to dig deeper to discover where and why you are tolerating people or circumstances that don't serve you. What situations in your daily life do you continue to tolerate that will result in no change whatsoever?

Ask yourself if this is how you would still like to be living six months from now?

What I now know:

- If you stop tolerating behaviors and people who do not serve you, you will be happier.
- If you take just five minutes and go within to see what you are tolerating or putting up with, and write them down, by bringing them to your awareness, you will be able to limit your tolerance in areas that do not serve your highest interests.
- Living a truly authentic life dissipates tolerance. Being authentic and living your truth is the opposite of tolerance.
- Let go of your tolerance when it does not serve you and be okay with it. Let it loose.
- You can stop living this way without major consequences by taking steps to limit what you tolerate in your life.

"Although an intolerable view is a 'negative' perspective, I believe it protects our self-respect. Certain people and environments need not be tolerated..."

-Anna Pereira, Circles of Inspiration

Questions to Ponder

- If I only had six months to live what one thing would I change that I'm currently tolerating?

- Where am I using avoidance or tolerance as a defense mechanism to get through a situation in my life right now?

- Who or what in my life am I tolerating?

- What area of my life is currently requiring the most tolerance?

- What does this relationship or circumstance bring to my life?

- Make a list of the personal, emotional, and financial cost of your tolerance in this area.

When we go inward with our feelings of tolerance, we're able to observe them, acknowledge them, and ultimately choose to be tolerant only if it will serve us. This awareness in itself will inspire change and our life will take on new meaning.

I get to choose when I want to allow tolerance to guide me. These feelings of self-preservation are the beginning signs of self-love, self-respect, and self-awareness of what is real for us. Time (of which hypothetically I have very little of) will tell.

WEEK 2: GETTING REAL IN MY RELATIONSHIPS

"Why wait for the funeral to say good things about someone, tell them NOW."

-*Martin Soulreader*

Most of us are living our lives daily with very demanding jobs. I'm blessed with three children and four grandchildren who I'd do anything for, a boyfriend who requires much of my attention, and a 105-year-old Grandmother, who I provide care and support for. Add to this a close relationship with four brothers, who are all uniquely intertwined in my life, my father who lives hours away, and a best friend or three in need of my support. And then there's Cathy. Who?

Enough said.

There are cupboards to clean because if I die someone is going to see them. There are finances to organize, because if I die someone needs to know. There's work to do, because if I die …

I suppose this is one way to look at it, but what keeps coming up for me is the quality of my relationships in this "relationship" filled life. What do my relationships with the people I love through all this busyness really look and feel like?

What am I getting and what am I giving in the relationships that I claim to value above all? I had a knowing feeling of how all of this would be so very important with six months to live. My home team, the people who keep me going, my tribe, the ones I help keep going, the ones who really know me. I decided to focus on them this week, and to feel into their importance in my life.

I noticed my daughter standing at the door the other night swearing she had forgot something and I thought, "a kiss goodbye" then she suddenly walked over and gave me the cheek to cheek like always. After cluttered thoughts, full of excuses, I had to tell my best friend the truth. I couldn't be there for her that day and I think I had one of the most meaningful phone conversations with her to date while we pondered the meaning of life. Never underestimate the value of a simple ten-minute honest phone conversation.

When my son's conversation seemed to linger for longer than usual, I noticed that sometimes even grown men need their mothers. My ailing Grandmother's tears of loneliness finally snapped me into action to take the time to call her every day and visit every week. When the news came from my beautiful niece calling to tell me her fiancé had been diagnosed with Hodgkin Lymphoma and that they were in for the fight of their lives, I stopped and made note that right now family was all they had to help them survive. #teammattevans

The realization that your interpersonal relationships are the single most important thing in your life can open your heart in unimaginable ways. You know who these people are; the people who cannot be replaced. The love you feel for each person you're in relationship with is unique, powerful, and irreplaceable.

The thick or thin, good or bad loyalty bond is what we live for. Family is usually there for family, and although it becomes more apparent during tragedy and trauma, that security alone should help someone tear down years of built up walls and turn years of family squabbling into dust.

Today I realize that if I have only six months to live, I want everybody who's important to me to know how important they are. I welcome the realization that not everybody I "do" for is in that circle when it comes down to it, and that may have been the hardest lesson in examining my real relationships.

Often we put other people or careers before our real relationships only to realize, often too late, that this is where our attention should be. We rush through our days communicating with a quick peck here and there, or a text that abbreviates an entire sentence. Sometimes we even use social media just to get in contact with a child.

We endlessly tell ourselves we have no time, and we rush, rush, rush. Busyness doesn't give us a pass to ignore the tribe, nor does it justify not stopping for long enough to tell someone they're loved. Can I really defend the cleaning or the franticness at work over the time I can spend and laugh with my most valued possessions? Is it rational to think that a work-related deadline is more important than another person's feelings? With six months to live, it was a resounding "NO."

Relationships take two people. We often forget that listening and absorbing what someone has to say is one of the most important things we can bring to a real relationship, and yet, often in our own need to be heard, we fail to hear what another person has to say, let alone find a way to acknowledge it. Sometimes I want to scream, "Is anybody listening to anybody?"

Abraham Hicks spiritual advisor to life said "Every time you are in a rush, slow down." This advice was life changing for me. I practice it every day and resist the rushed anxiety from flowing to me knowing that life is too short to be in a hurry. If I'm rushing through moments instead of being in them I know I'm missing out on life and the lives of the people I'm in relationships with.

Whenever I've stopped for long enough to really share the joy in someone's successes or notice that they're passively seeking my advice or opinion and I give it, lives are changed. Both theirs and mine.

Every year on my birthday I make a CD that tells a story of my year through music and I pass it out to my dearest friends. It started rather innocently as a party favor one year. Now it's something I look forward to every year because I always learn something about myself in the process. Years later when I hear that year's CD and I get the musical time lapse into my soul, I'm always so happy that I created this ritual in my life and that I have a posse of people to share it with.

I want the people who need me at times in their lives to know that I'm here for them, and I want to know the same thing about them. Because what it boils down to is having people in your life who you can trust with your life. That has to be a reciprocal process. It requires a knowing trust for another soul, and when you know it, you know it.

There's great impact when you let people know you love them, no matter what.

We go through our life having many encounters with many people. How many of them are you in a real relationship with? With whom in your life do you get to be just you with? This became a vital and intricate part of living my life as if each day mattered. When I have to fake it to get through a conversation with someone, or if I've tuned out and can't answer the question in front of me because I wasn't listening, everybody starts to get uncomfortable. I want to show up every time, with every person, as who I am, and I want to be connected. Connection is the most rewarding experience two people can have.

Real relationships require work. They require tuning in and listening skills a lot of us don't have. They require eye contact. I've had conversations with people where I've been looking at them pretending to listen, or vice-versa, and been really uncomfortable at the fact that we've both known it. You have to put the phone down to be in a real relationship.

In order to change this for myself I had to get real. I had to stop thinking the thoughts in my head and tune in to the person with all my energy. Being present is a massive gift we can give others and ourselves. Just for one second stop and take a breath. In through the nose, out through the mouth, and feel for a moment. Feel what a moment of life feels like.

In every conversation you have throughout the next week, try to listen without thinking random thoughts, and be present with each person. When a text comes in during your conversation, don't look at your phone. When a notification comes in, look away. When a call comes in, unless it's important, hit silent and be present in your relationship.

When dinner rolls around, have everybody throw their phones in the basket or turn them off. Talk to each other and find out what's going on in the life of someone else.

Before cell phones, when my kids were growing up, we had a dinnertime ritual where we'd go around the table and say our highs and lows. This was inspired after watching the movie "The Story of Us" about a family on the verge of divorce. I found out more about my children in those conversations than at any other time in their lives, because for that moment, when they were relaying their highs and their lows of just one day, they had to get real.

A real relationship is felt at a visceral level. It feels so good to know that someone loves you, cares enough to listen, and truly values who you are. When I leave this planet, you're going to know that we were in a real relationship because I was there, and I'm going to know that same thing about you. Important stuff.

Questions to Ponder

- If I only had six months to live, whom would I want to know how much they mean to me? DO NOT WAIT ONE MORE MINUTE - TELL THEM

- Whom would I want to help?

- Whom do I need to tell something to that has gone unsaid for far too long?

- Who is the number one person in my life that is unconditionally afforded my time without feeling guilty, in a rush or regret? (Remember that name)

- Who makes me feel joy?

- Who brings me down? (Forget those names)

- Who is the most important person to me?

- When am I making time to tell/show them?

Does everyone in your inner world really know what his or her relationship means to you?

Today let them know. Today live and love with six months to live.

WEEK 3: THE JOY JUMPS

"I just want to spend the rest of my life laughing."
-Author unknown

Ask yourself, Where does your joy come from? Where is your happy place?

I love homecoming week. It takes me back to a place I often feel I may have been centuries ago. I feel joy at the homecoming rally that for years had me sneaking in to watch my cheerleader daughter perform. I feel joy at the parade that runs down the main drag, trucks filled with screaming enthusiastic kids dressed in their chosen color. I feel joy at the halftime routine, perfectly choreographed by the students. I cry with whichever class wins the spirit bell.

I'm filled with joy at the sight of three hundred kids in the middle of a football field holding hands and running into the middle together. I remember, and it stays etched in my mind, the night my daughter performed for the last time.

I had expected to have this huge emotional breakdown; a nostalgic ending of sorts, but aghast, nothing. No tears, no feeling. I couldn't figure this out. I momentarily stepped back to ask myself where the numbness was coming from. Maybe it was because my daughter had warned me it was her last year even though I begged her to step outside of herself and do it for "me" one more year to no avail, or maybe I'd just run cold at the thought of endings.

What was the unemotional feeling I was feeling? When I dissected the day, I remembered that I'd cried tears of joy that morning when

I took the girls' picture in their spirit clothes and drove away. I cried tears of joy when I left the rally knowing I'd just left "my baby" girl at her high school rally for the last time, and that her whole life was ahead of her.

I cried tears of joy at the parade before it even started as I held my newest grandchild while he anticipated his first parade with excitement.

While tears may indicate many different emotions or feelings, tears of joy are like a beam of light that shines through us and produces a different kind of cry. Tears that warm your heart instead of hurting it. I'd spent so much time recently crying hurt tears that I'd forgotten what tears of joy felt like. Joy is truly beyond compare.

Joy is momentary. We feel it in moments when it comes into our center and we well up with joy tears, or when we're tuned in enough to feel that personal knowing inside (I call it 'the joy jump'). There's no other feeling like it. That inner jump is the moment you know you are in alignment with yourself in the truest sense. Joy is one of the biggest gifts of life. In order to feel this beautiful emotion called joy simply pick up a baby or play with young children. They live in almost a constant state of joy and excitement. Any new mother or father knows the feeling of joy when they finally meet their newborn child. Joy is also present when we celebrate the successes in our lives.

I'd gone through a deflating experience that suffocated my joy channel, and I was unable to feel anything, let alone joy. Days would pass by where I'd miss out on leading an enriched life while I wallowed in my story. Every person I ran into heard the "woes" about what had happened to me. Psychic, Collete Barron Reid, during a Hay House World Summit interview in 2015 described it perfectly for me with her expression, "…like walking around with your story suction cupped to your face." Post-Traumatic Stress (PTSD) from this experience ruled my everyday life. Seeking professional help for PTSD, my therapist suggested an exercise for thirty days that opened me up to a joy I'd never discovered before: self-joy – doing things for me that made me happy.

This exercise involved me spending two hours each day doing something for myself that brought me joy. It seemed simple enough until I had to segregate what joy really felt like. In these moments I met myself for maybe the first time. It involved singing with my grandson repeatedly until we both knew every word, or reading a great book by the pool for two hours straight with no interruptions, or hiking alone in the redwoods, or a mid-afternoon fancy wine filled lunch with a friend. It involved bike riding or meditating, painting my nails and toes, wearing makeup, shopping, beach walks, counting stars, or simply sitting in my hammock in complete nothingness.

I was required to start the day meditating, which was difficult for me. I've always been a thinker beyond what's safe, and before this process started I was a constant worrier. This made it difficult to find joy. Once I started to feel joy again, it was as if a fire ignited inside of me. I became aware of where in my life I wasn't feeling any semblance of joy. I became aware of who was suffocating my joy channels, or in other words, who was raining on my parade. It was such a revelation. Once I started to feel joy again I chased the joyous moments, grabbing them wherever and whenever I could, and thanking them for the ability to feel again.

I became aware that being in my joy was where I felt the best. I realized that I could smile every day and honestly be happy for myself and others who were living in their state of joy. We aren't here on this planet to feel bad. We aren't here to feel guilt. We aren't here to be the judge or be judged. We aren't here to silence somebody else, instill fear, or intimidate others. All of these character traits choke the joy right out of us.

Helping someone else is a surefire way to ignite this feeling. Whenever I see the work of The Make A Wish Foundation© I'm in awe of the joy they bring into the lives of people who have terminal illnesses.

Handing out Fast Passes (to get on rides in half the time) at Disneyland to people who had been standing in line for two hours was priceless. (the look of joy on their faces was worth the admission price)

Who doesn't love a parade? Glee, clapping, joy, and smiling faces everywhere!

Everyone's joy is different. When you find yours, you'll understand fully. Joy is that brief moment when you well up with tears and you sit with it for long enough to feel the warmth in your heart, the invisible sunshine on your face, and a feeling of complete bliss.

That is the feeling that can change the world. I know that not all of us have the time to take two hours as I did. So instead take ten minutes or as long as your schedule allows. Do something for you that brings you joy every day, and then it will become your pattern. It works. I was organically changed as a result. The post-traumatic stress transformed into post-traumatic growth. According to Davidji, a meditation teacher at the Chopra Center in Carlsbad, California and renowned author on stress, post-traumatic growth is a growing trend; a condition that's only now being recognized as such. As people begin to awaken from the deep debilitating stages of PTSD, from the depths of their soul, they will acquire a different mindset and begin to find the positive side of the tragic situations that created their past trauma. Finding joy in everyday life assists in climbing out of these negative feelings into feelings that resurrect inner peace and bliss.

When I understood that, everything changed for me. I now seek joy in my life every day. Nowadays I don't go through a day without experiencing a 'joy jump,' and when I do, I welcome it with delight. For example, "Hmmm, what was that delightful feeling? I recognize and I give thanks for it. Seeking joy at this level becomes something you can't *not* do anymore. It will affect you at a gut level and it will never be an issue again because it's my belief that once you know what brings you joy, you're wired to follow it.

"Remember that joy is your natural state"

-Dr. Wayne Dyer

17

Questions to Ponder

- What am I doing in my daily life that brings me joy?

- What does my joy look like to me?

- What one thing can I do for myself each day that brings me joy?

- Who in my life brings me the most joy and why?

- Am I helping others feel joy, or am I the habitual buzz kill? (In addition, if you are a joy kill, stop it!)

- Identify where you are adding joy and where you are allowing others to take your joy away.

- Where have I put joy in my life as a first priority?

- Ask yourself, when do I let joy fly by without really experiencing it?

When you know joy, you know there's no other possible feeling that compares to how you should always feel inside. It's a natural high that you can't get from a drink or a drug, but it's very addicting and there's no other high I need.

'Joy is your barometer to a very happy life"

-Pam Grout

WEEK 4: DE-STRESS YOURSELF

"I have got 99 problems, and 86 of them are completely made up scenarios in my head that I am stressing about for absolutely no logical reason."

-Author unknown − Calm Down Now app

I had a very hard time finding my groove today. I felt that feeling of upset or nervousness you cannot shake away. No matter how hard I tried, I wasn't feeling that authenticity so important in our life. Maybe it's because I've come to realize that I've been living in a constant state of nervousness. I seem to be more concerned about pleasing my anxious housemates than myself. The fight about whether the dog should or shouldn't be on the bed. The daughters who after years of being raised under my watchful eye are happy to be free and run wild, but they have not conquered real life yet. Worrying if the career choices of my sons will make it in this unpredictable world. I can't shake these thoughts. When you add a highly stressful job environment to the equation, which completely eats your brain, all of these elements bring an energy I wish to eliminate.

If I could.

With the six months to live theory, if none of those things mattered anymore how would I feel on a Monday? This became the looming question. What would my "chosen way" of everyday life look like? For giggles, I took this challenge and wrote it all down on paper. I had no idea that by doing this simple exercise I'd begin to live these type of days, whatever day of the week it was.

I wake up slowly on my own personal inner clock – naturally. No alarms allowed.

Silence is the first thing I hear besides the chirping of birds.

I drink a strong coffee.

I go for a brisk walk and listen to someone with more wisdom than I on everyday coping skills in order to stay in touch with myself.

I quietly meditate while I soak in the outdoor elements and I say a prayer for those I love. I don't worry about money, people, or what I have to do tomorrow. I look at my calendar and greet my tasks with delight. I work on my passion to bring light to a dark world.

I watch a little television, always GMA. I head to the gym for Pilates or Yoga, drink a green smoothie, lunch outside or with a good friend, enjoy an afternoon writing session, walk the dog, and prep for some home cooked dinner with a glass of dark red wine. I start a fire in the fireplace or a BBQ just for the smell, and be ready to greet my family with grace and love.

POP! BEEEEEP! WAKE UP! Reality check time!

That would be an ideal Monday, but that isn't how it happened on most Mondays in my life.

JOURNAL ENTRY: *I woke up with scowls, like every Monday with the thought of going to my job. There's no question in my mind that if I woke up on a deserted beach I'd be happiest. Instead of being leisurely, I hightail it out of there like a bobcat running for his life, just so I don't have to remember the fact that it's only Monday. I race to the gym for a quick thirty-minute run. I race back to my house, take a quick shower, and rush to pick up my granddaughter to get her to school on time. I race to the office where I go through four hundred emails that mean nothing to me and I take no time for lunch. After a bazillion interruptions (noting that nothing has been accomplished as a result), I'm off to the supermarket where four hundred other people are shopping with the same lack of exuberance as I. I then race home to start dinner, eat, do the dishes, prepare some coffee, make lunch for tomorrow, and then finally I have a moment to relax. Meme and I watching my favorite reality TV family of sisters living their lives late into the night, so I can forget about mine.*

Ironically, or rather expectedly, this became the highlight of my day.

Clearly I wasn't living my dream day.

Stress is the million-dollar phrase these days. "I'm so stressed out." "I can't handle all the stress." "Please stop talking, you're stressing me out." "What are you stressed about?" "Stop stressing." There are stress reduction workshops, hypnosis centers knocking it out of your life with the power of suggestion, stress clinics, stress tests…Stress, stress, stress, stress. What is it really?

According to Wikipedia, *"Physiological or biological stress is an organism's response to a stressor, such as an environmental condition or a stimulus. Stress is the body's method of reacting to a challenge. According to the stressful event, the body's way to respond to stress is by sympathetic nervous system activation, which results in the fight-or-flight response. In humans, stress typically describes a negative condition or a positive condition that can have an impact on a person's mental and physical well-being."*

Stress is a physiological response to a stressor. Okay, so what is a stressor?

A stressor is:

Like being stuck in traffic when you're already late, losing your keys, your glasses, and your cell phone for the ninth time only to then find them in the most obvious place.

Life changes are stressors: moving, divorce, loss of a job, children moving out, and the death of a loved one, betrayal.

We get daily stressor responses stemming from the demands of our jobs, particularly when people come at you with extreme postures to control your every move at work.

Alcohol or drug use is a huge stressor on your nervous system, which triggers your loved ones to stress about you. That, in turn, makes you feel guilty, which in addition stresses you out.

Thoughts can be huge stressors and the funny thing is they aren't even REAL!

"Stress" is the biggest circle (cluster) of neurons in your body. These neurons trigger off each other until your nervous system is so banged up that YOU CAN'T TAKE IT ANYMORE.

After you've reached the point where it's no longer endurable you can only hope it's not too late; that your heart muscle and blood flow hasn't been damaged, that your arteries are not clogged, that the cortisol isn't stuck, and that your gray hairs aren't falling out. You silently pray that you can lose the weight you gained by not going to the gym because you were too "stressed."

How do you know you're there? Because you begin to have physical reactions to what once affected you only on a physiological (tolerable) level. Because your clothes are packed and you're in the car throwing out the rearview mirror.

You may shake at the sound of someone's stern voice, or loud noises, such as a dog barking. A horn honk will startle you.

You may feel closed in at times in large crowds or start to hear ringing in your ears. You may feel toxic as if something is always wrong. BECAUSE SOMETHING IS. YOU ARE STRESSING OUT!

Once you get to this point, I promise there's no going back. Your body simply doesn't let you function without a constant physical reminder. You know the ailments, "Oh, my neck hurts, and my aching back." You get constant colds, and sickness. "Grrrrrrrr" becomes a second language. You understand the meaning of the sound of fingernails on a chalkboard all too clearly. You roll your eyes and mutter a lot.

When someone comes at me during the day with negative ions, I sweep their energy away from my path and I do not allow myself to absorb it. I know that if I can't handle my own day, I certainly can't handle yours. I've learned that the nicest thing I can do for a stressed out person is be silent, and move along.

What I want you to know is that had I listened to these signs in their beginning stages I wouldn't have been one of the ones who had to radically shift. I could have made the changes slowly and in my own time, as I learned how to cope and stay balanced to live an authentic life. And trust me, the universe will eventually force it upon you if you don't see if for yourself.

Today I shared the following quote, accompanied by a photo of a beautiful glass swimming pool against the infinity of the ocean, and the back of a woman, dressed in white, gazing outward. She was sitting in the meditation posture embracing the beautiful scene in front of her. It was taken from the realbeautiful.ca Facebook web page. After reading this quote, how could you not want to meditate?

"Why do we meditate?

...to decrease depression, cortisol, adrenaline, to increase expansion, consciousness, insight, intuition, immunity, balance hormones in our bodies, clarify our focus, improve our mood, improve our confidence, decrease our addictions, fear, negative thoughts, to increase our success, abundance, prosperity, beauty, uplift our energy vibration and that of others, to spread ripples of peace, to heal ourselves, others and the world, to make contact with heaven, and create miracles..."

Meditation and breathing is the only way I know to bring you to living in the moment. Breath is the only thing that helps me to escape the madness. One of the most important things I learned on my journey to live as if each day mattered was to start my day in silence and completely empty my mind of any negative thoughts. This one practice put me in touch with my inner truths in ways I couldn't have predicted. It also calmed my otherwise frantic personality and forced me to concentrate on what was important about the day in front of me. Here's the kicker – it only takes you ten minutes to achieve this state of being. If you take just ten minutes a day or ten minutes when you're "stressed out," you'll change the neurons in your body from frantic to peaceful and quickly activate the ability to de-stress. My good friend Leah spoke to me about how her stressful lifestyle almost led to her death and she has graciously shared her story with us.

Leah's Story:

Today marks one year since my heart attack. A Coronary Vasospasm is not caused from heart disease, it's caused by stress or smoking. At forty-six years old, I never dreamed this would end up as part of my story. As a recovering alcoholic who's nine years sober, I've been saved from death's door twice. For both, I'm forever grateful. As a result, I've made some healthy changes both emotionally and physically, and I continue to do so. I'm a different person today than I was last year. I've grown so much and I've found a hunger inside to grow even more. I've always been an over achiever, very structured, OCD, intense, and a stress case. I've slowly learned that everything important will get done, and if not, it will still be there tomorrow. If I'm gone from this earth and it isn't done, does it really matter? On the other hand, if I'm gone and my time with loved ones or our adventures were put aside to conquer my to-do list, am I really living a fulfilled life? Nothing is worth stressing over and wasting a precious day. Nothing. I know this today. I know we can control our mind and our expectations. Some of my best days are the ones where I push everything on my list to the side and simply be present with my loved ones.

Some days I need a nothing day or an unexpected fun day with family or friends.

Today I'm able to do that guilt free. I'm present in all I do in mind, body, and spirit. I've always been a giver to all in need, yet when the heart attack hit, I found that my priorities weren't directed to the ones I love. I could have run a class on People Pleasing 101. Learning to say no was a healthy change. The people I love the most are the ones I spend my energy and time with now. This is where my soul is fed. I've found balance through my awareness. I know we're not going to live forever. When coming face to face with it, it's an undeniable fact. Things I used to put off, I've chosen to now do or plan. I have a deep desire to live.

Recently I was lucky enough to accompany my eighty-eight year old Grandmother to Disneyland for her first trip ever with my fifteen and twenty year old sons. I'm unable to put into words how amazing, rewarding, and nourishing to the soul those four days were for all. I'm also lucky enough to have spent seven full days and nights caring for my Mother who had knee

25

replacement surgery this month; another amazing nourishment for the soul. My health has never been a big one for me. I've never been obese or horribly unhealthy, yet I've always eaten whatever I wish. I've been known to eat very little due to busy days and nights. At the time of my heart attack, I was at my lowest weight in years but truly thought I felt great. I do believe my nutrition along with stress, played key roles in that darn coronary vasospasm. Now ten pounds heavier, I eat more often and I eat much healthier foods (although there's the occasional binge to keep me happy). I'm hoping to find a balance in my nutrition, and I'm still working on that one. Spirituality is now huge for me. It's so important for me to live day to day with a grateful heart and mind, and I must stay connected. Nature and babies seem to be a connection for me. The birds, sky, forest, and the ocean always remind me of how small I truly am on this planet. A baby's smile, laughter, smell, and tiny little toes remind me how amazing and fragile life is. These take me out of myself and allow me to connect spiritually with my Creator.

Yet, even with this awareness, in all honesty, some days I can be two seconds away from an anxiety attack. I've learned my triggers and all I can say is that I'm better today than I was yesterday at controlling my stress and worries. We'll never know why some people live long healthy lives while some people die far too young, but I'm certain that it's quality not quantity. I'm not sure what tomorrow will bring or even what this evening will bring so I truly live from experience. I have to enjoy every moment I'm given. I'm fortunate enough to have a spouse who keeps me in check, as I do for him, when fading to that poor me place. The closeness that a near death experience brings to a couple and your loved ones is the silver lining that comes out of an experience such as this.

This experience created a need to find a balance of love, giving of ourselves compassionately, fun, adventure, comfort, spirituality, and enjoying the luxuries of life. I think we might have found the key to a happy life and a full and happy memory bank. That, my friends is my daily goal! I've had many grateful days in my lifetime but I must say thinking today about all I might have missed in this last year fills my heart and soul with an amount of gratefulness I've never felt before. I'm blessed and forever grateful to spend more of my life and my days with my loves.

Leah Mendoza

Questions to Ponder

- If I only have six months to live, what's so important that I need to rush it? (Unless you are racing to the hospital for the birth of your child, the answer is nothing.)

- What belief about myself has been guiding me to believe that there is a strict time frame for everything, and that if I don't complete it in this structured time I have given myself, I have somehow failed?

- Why do I put expectations on myself and say yes?

- What stops me from saying NO?

- What one shift can I make in my daily life to reduce stressors?

- Identify three areas of your life that bring you the most stress.

- Name one action for each of those three areas that you can do to eliminate some of the stress they bring:

ASK YOURSELF:

When is now going to be enough for me without the worry of the future or the consequence?

Now. Now is enough. This may have been the hardest lesson for me to date, but I guarantee if you stop the madness and allow your days to go with the flow of life, as Eckhart Tolle so eloquently puts it, "As if you have chosen it," it is life changing. It's enough to stop you in your tracks and show you that:

You have chosen it, which makes you very observant and selective of your choices. We need to accept each moment of our lives as if we have chosen it and go with it, without one drop of resistance. Then, suddenly the stressful part of everything you do will disappear.

I believe that nothing is random. Too many events, circumstances, and people I have encountered in my life have proven this to me. We will all be able to look back on our lives with a distinct knowing that nothing is random, so why fight it?

Every person, place, job, meet up or break up has led me to the next event almost seamlessly. It's a fact that I, nor I believe any of us, can ignore. When it becomes a chosen moment and you disassociate time with it, it becomes something you're doing instead of the stressful OMG rattle inside. You exchange it for the peace of knowing you're right where you're supposed to be.

Goodbye timeframes, hello life. Take the "how do I want my life to look everyday" challenge and start striving for the life you want to live! De-stress yourself.

We never know where the most profound sparks in our life will come from, or who will strike that match. Sparks fly out of nowhere.

-Caroline Myss

MONTH 2

WEEK 5: CHANGE

"Sometimes the things we can't change end up changing us."

-My daughter

UCSF, San Francisco, California 2003

Twelve years ago, I lived in every parent's worst nightmare. My daughter was stricken with an incurable disease that they could not diagnose for several weeks. We were blessed enough to spend thirty-one days in the most prestigious children's hospital in Northern California and our lives were organically changed.

Theory says it takes twenty-one days to change a habit. When you live your daily life in a hospital, you grow to love and experience an unexplainable style of living. You gain global understanding about human life, witness other people's hardship and faith, and you change forever. When you witness the massive strength and resilience of parents nurturing and cheering on their sick children, while inside juggling other children and jobs, you're never the same. We spent those thirty-one days in a children's cancer ward.

We met children with terminal cancers and livers that weren't working. We watched parents drop to their knees in grief at the news they had just heard. We watched as mothers cried and fathers stoically held it together. We watched one family with an eleven month old little boy who had a liver transplant and had to stay there for nine months. Every night at 6pm, they would pull him around the ward in a red wagon and with his favorite blanket in his hand they would stop at our door for a visit. He loved my daughter and it brought her a lesson in the simple joy of a baby's smile. He always bounced with joy when he saw her. They gave each other a silent gift with the simple exchange of smiles in a pretty scary place. The parents of this child were humble, polite, and fearless of their future.

The only thing that mattered to them was that on that day Jonathan was still alive.

We cried, we played, we ate delicious cuisine, we wrote a gratitude journal every day, and we bonded in a way I could never bond with anyone else. We watched my favorite soap opera, All My Children, at noon everyday laughing about their problems, and totally forgetting about our own. We had conversations about Greenlee and Ryan, the famous stars of the show, as if they were our friends. By the end of our stay, nurses would position themselves in our room promptly at noon with any excuse to come in and out and catch what was now "their soap too."

We fell in love with strangers and we didn't want to leave some of them. We hugged everyone almost daily and loved people in a way we never knew existed.

Knowing that they were just a person quickly passing through our lives, yet knowing they had made a place in our hearts forever was bittersweet. I know that I'll never forget this experience, nor could I expect anyone to understand how this experience changed us.

But it did.

Life has a way of bringing us to our knees in order to make some changes. We're so afraid of making them ourselves that we wait until unexplainable universal events lead us to the change, most times kicking and screaming. It always feels so much safer to stay where you are in life. I had been forging on in an unfulfilling relationship, working three jobs to make ends meet, and I still couldn't pay my mortgage. Things were beginning to spiral out of control. Those thirty-one days were the stopping point for many unworkable things in my life.

Big changes usually follow a big event that brings your life crashing down around you. In one moment all rationale overtakes the spirit's desires *(that is the true driving force inside)* and we go on these really long stints of unworkable life *(deep down knowing it isn't working)*, and when we get our wake-up call we fall to our knees asking why? Ironically, if we'd followed the feeling on the inside, the knowing that things weren't working, and fearlessly made the changes needed, we probably could have bypassed a measure of life's untimely schooling. When you make a change of your own freewill, from a knowing empowered place, you unleash the barriers that hold you back from living and following the life you deserve to be living. You understand that when change appears it's always for your highest good and you follow that path like your life depends on it.

Every eight weeks we return to this hospital for a drug curing infusion and I pride at the tenacity of my daughter's ability to stay calm. When I'm there, I also get a very familiar sense of peace come over me. My time here twelve years ago forced my usual busy self to stop and look at our life, to look at my priorities and choices. Parenting moved to the forefront of my life and without a doubt it became one of the biggest "bless-ons" I've ever had. Life had to change because I didn't have the balls to change it myself.

Does it take life's banging hammer to make us see what isn't working? Why do we wait for wake-up calls to make changes we already know we need? Do we have to wait for an illness, a fire, to be fired, or to have an accident to show us? Does it take a six month to live life sentence to teach me to let go of the reins and start living? I had contemplated this many times since then. I hoped not.

Time, again, would be my only teller and I theoretically had only a bit left.

Today I look at what isn't working once again, only now knowing the universal crash that will ultimately happen if I wait to change. I've learned to take the time to evaluate my life and note where it isn't working. I allow myself the awareness that if it isn't working I do not need to keep trying to put a circle into a square hole.

Rather than fear change, I've learned to embrace it. I know that change is the way I evolve and grow. I used to fear every projection of change I saw, wanting to keep everything in the neat little package I had wrapped. That isn't real life though. Real life is constantly changing. This is when I learned you have to go with the flow of change. When things are changing, buckle up and take the ride, because I can honestly say that without it I'd feel nowhere near the level of excitement I now feel every day.

Change is inevitable and it's a constant force in our lives. Whenever I find myself in the midst of change, I grip it. I'm no longer afraid of what the future might bring because I know my choices are what make it. I look for the best things I can, and I stay convicted that I'm being called to these changes for my highest good. I simply go with the flow.

Today as I sit at UCSF and hear the little progress her disease has made towards a cure, I go back to that thirty-one days. I remind myself that it's now time to change what isn't working in my life, and I don't need another thirty-one day sentence to prove that to myself.

Questions to Ponder

- If you were diagnosed with an incurable disease, what immediate changes would you make in your life?

- What's happening in your life right now that you know deep down isn't working?

- How would you feel and/or treat a loved one diagnosed with an incurable disease?

- What one thing can you name that isn't working in your life that you have been avoiding?

- Name your needed change.

- What's stopping you from making this change?

- List the positive ways a change like this would change your life.

Ask yourself: Every time a change has happened that I was afraid of, did it turn out to be the best or the worst thing that ever happened? Nine out of ten times, it will be the best. I have heard many people say to me:

"If that hadn't happened I wouldn't be here now."

WEEK 6: THE R-WORD

REGRET– RESENTMENT-RAGE-REVENGE

> *"Holding grudges. Judging others. Hating. Wanting to cause harm. Withholding forgiveness. Gossiping. Ridiculing. Ignoring others. Withholding mercy. Throwing stones. Stop it."*
>
> *-Dieter J. Uchtdorf*

Life is too short to allow any of these useless emotions to hold you back from living a life of pure joy.

Regret usually creeps in when you're alone or when you see the path a different choice would have taken you down. Regret lives underneath your present moments. It shows itself in your mind's eye and before you know it, your emotions begin chiming in.

Pictures play back in your mind to show scenes from the life you had, or tears stream down your face in a black streak of mascara when you remember the pivotal day you made that life defining choice, much to your regret. These are moments when you shouldn't have, should have, feelings of despair, outrage, what you wished you'd done, or said, or hadn't done or said.

When you blew the one shot you had to change it all.

Days can't be unwritten. In everyone's life, there is something we will regret; a moment that changed the world for you or someone else forever. I have a regret. I keep it locked away so deep that I didn't even know it myself until today.

Thirty-three years ago, I left my home in one minute, on one day, when I'd had enough. I grabbed only the possessions I could carry: a beat up old station wagon, my baby and his baby clothes, a VCR, and two hundred dollars I dug out of my drug induced, passed out husband's pocket.

I went "home," I confessed the drug crazed life I'd been living, and asked my Mother for help. Fast forward five years after a bitter custody dispute over money and moving 150 miles away, he decided he didn't want to be a Dad anymore. The fight with me was over and we barely saw him again. In that time, he had a daughter, a sister to my son. The only time they ever spoke was twenty years later when she called to tell him that their Father had died three months earlier. He'd gone for a visit, left a note, and found out his Father was dead from a sister he never knew. There was no funeral and no closure. He had gone without any understanding as to why this man had stopped being his Dad.

I thought that it was my fault for a long time, but even I don't have that much power. We make choices in life and there's always a response from the universe regarding that choice. It was his choice, not mine, but I regret it anyway. His will was weak. His pride and his way of life choices came first.

Today, however, threw my emotions for a loop. I received a phone call and when the voice on the other end said...

Her: *"I know this is random, but do you have a son named - ?"*
Me: *"Who is this?"*
Her: *"-name-"*
ME: *"last name?"* And then the biggest "OH MY GOD" poured from my mouth and every cell in my body changed. I was so overwhelmed with emotions of all kinds that I'd never experienced anything like it. Here on this random day out of nowhere was the sister my son had never met, calling me. Later that day they connected in a parking lot as she drove through our small town. She cried as she looked at her brother who was a spitting image of the father she had lost. There were no words, just several years of regret.

God works in mysterious ways and I try not to overlook universal gifts that can provide healing.

What do you regret the most about your life? Looking at "six months to live" it struck me that I had so many more regrets than I anticipated, and I pondered why I felt these overwhelming feelings. What had led me to make those choices? And worse yet, was it too late for a redo? Almost, always. However, I found that if I sat and listed every stinking regret I could begin to unravel the whys, the how to from here, and the never do again!

I went back as far as I could.

For every regret I have, I could write a chapter, why it happened, and what I had learned. However, I'll share just the brunt of my list. When I sat down to write it, I went with whatever thought came next. It's my hope that you will do the same. Next, I'll burn the list on the night of a full moon, with candles, and angels to help let it all go.

I regret stealing the huge poor boy statue from the beautiful garden across the street from our family home on the day we made the move from the big city to the suburbs. I was nine years old. That statue had been my friend on the days when the other kids wouldn't play with me. We talked, sang, conspired, and laughed together me and that statue, and I took him because even though he belonged to the poor woman whose yard I took it from, in my eyes he was mine.

I can't imagine what the owner of that house thought when she walked into her garden. I also can't imagine how I slipped it through my mother's ever-suspicious eyes. I regret it because it was stealing, and by it being okay at the age of nine, stealing became far too easy. There were many moments after that where I took things that weren't mine, all I might add, that I was caught for.

I regret always trying to be somebody else in order to fit in, which led to a lifetime of never feeling accepted.

I regret the first moment that I talked back to my Mother, which set up a relationship that was barely salvaged before she died.

I regret my first cigarette, joint, drink, and drug, and the fact that my parents didn't grab me by the hair and ship me off to boarding school when those behaviors surfaced at the age of fourteen.

I regret never giving myself time to get over one boyfriend before I had another. How I accomplished this as I look back over my life I'll never know. My first real boyfriend was at the age of fourteen and it lasted until I was twenty. I've had a total of twelve months since then when I was single.

I regret not getting to know myself better as a result. I spent a lot of time living someone else's life.

I regret not exercising every single day.

I regret not spending enough time with my grandmothers and absorbing their wisdom, from cooking, to knitting, to life with nothing. There will always be a generation gap, but if you read between the lines when you hear your great elders talk, they know their stuff.

I regret not listening and thinking I knew it all.

I regret the friendships I never gave a chance because I thought they were beneath me.

I regret ever being a mean girl. There was one person I was especially mean to, and I regret that every day.

I regret that I hurt people without thinking. I regret the choices I made unconsciously. They were the most lethal.

I regret that my tendency to deal with things involved shutting off and detaching rather than expressing and communicating my truth. I probably would have lost a lot of unnecessary weight and cleared the path of all the toxic waste I let linger.

I regret that I always said yes.

I regret that I never said no.

RESENTMENT

Resentment is one of the most wasted emotions on the planet. Unlike regret, resentment burns us from the inside out. Resentment is the emotion I describe as like a blood sucking insect living inside of you. If you're resentful of a person or because of an event in your life, stop and ask yourself where you have played a role. No one else is responsible for how you feel but you. Asking myself this question helped to clear my resentment up. For many years, I was very resentful of a certain person who was wreaking havoc in my daily life and I couldn't see the damage it was doing to me.

Interestingly, I barely knew her. However, each week she would creep into my daily existence with a memory of her wickedness or an unresolved emotion for other people in my life that I was unable to do anything about, but witness. She wasn't even my problem but I watched her do things to hurt and destroy people I loved with her lies and manipulation. I had zero power to change the situation for them, so I built up resentment, and one day when I could take no more evil thoughts about her, I had to look at what my part was in all this.

Part of my learning was that it was none of my business. The other part was that I had to realize that sometimes in life we can't save the world. And I cannot control the outcome for somebody else, only for myself, and only sometimes.

These resentments do not go away on their own. You have to identify them and spray yourself down so that you're completely untouched by other people's stuff. It helps to walk around with an invisible bubble around you to avoid being vacuumed into another person's energy field. When you're an empath that isn't always easy.

If you're resentful about something you have nowhere to look but at yourself. When I had this feeling about this person it would feel like a burning sensation. My whole body started to clench and feel stiff.

I asked myself, 'How is this helping me to live a life that mattered?' 'What good does it do me to sit around and resent what "you did" to me or worse still, to take on what you did to them?'

Here is a concept: *"LET IT GO. You're taking away from yourself and the simplicity of living life."*

Resentment leads you down one path, and one path only. It brings you right to:

RAGE

I wanted to add the concept of rage here because having studied the emotional scale of feelings presented by Abraham Hicks, anger, rage, revenge and hatred run simultaneously. And they will ruin your life. Do whatever you can to not allow rage to rule your life. This one single emotion will destroy any possibility of living a life that matters.

Rage is similar to a drug that runs through your veins. Your blood starts to boil and you can actually feel it swelling up. Your veins get bigger, your eyes pop out, your throat becomes dry, and your heart begins to accelerate. I have often thought I was losing consciousness in a rage fit. Have you ever watched someone's rage start to build? It's like watching the Incredible Hulk grow in front of your eyes. Words come out far louder than anyone needs to hear and you can't stop yourself. It's scary. Rage most often leads to the next emotion on the scale:

REVENGE

Once you have reached rage, revenge seems like the only way out. You want this person you are directing the rage at to feel hurt, suffer and slither and squirm, and feel like $H!T.

I know, as I've been there. Every time I wanted revenge it was because the rage inside was too much to handle and revenge was the only ticket out. I'd engage in extended thought processes of revenge and make up scenes of things happening to them as if I was writing for a television show. They suffer and I walk away the winner. Revenge lives in a dark corner of your mind.

Magically, through my work with my life coach, I went a long time without feeling rage and something wonderful happened. Life felt easy. I became aware that when my buttons were pushed in this direction, I had the option to detach with love for this person and realize that I'm not here to take on the world's problems. I was so proud that I'd managed to reach this mindset.

Then one day a situation arose out of nowhere and all my "good me" training went out of the window with one visit from Rage. Somebody had told a lie about me.

It was about to cost me thousands of dollars and the lie about me had been built from her "resentment" towards me! I sat there for about five minutes, official letter in hand, and then I got in my car and raged across town to confront the lies. When my raging tantrum and attempt to rationalize this person was done, I was not so politely "asked" to leave and I did, but not until I'd raged the word "b!TC&" to her including some other obscenities.

Then I wrote the scathing response letter that stated the truth, mailed it, and let it go. Had I done that first, I may have saved myself some embarrassment. As a result of acting this way I was completely off my game for five days. I noticed the difference between feeling peaceful and feeling full of rage. I noticed that I had reacted instead of responded.

I knew I had to let it go and let the universe handle the logistics. I'd be fine because the truth always comes out on top. But the looming question of why I, with everything I knew, couldn't allow the situation to resolve without rage became the number one thing I wanted to work on. I couldn't afford rage in my life anymore. I realized that if I allowed my rage responses to win every time I felt like I'd been wronged; I was going to rob myself of emotions that made me feel good instead of like I was being boxed into a corner. I also had to identify where all three of these emotions came splashing into my life to take away from a quality of life I knew I had to live from now on for survival.

I made a commitment to myself that every time I felt rage or anger about somebody or something I'd put it into the "will this matter in six months?" test. This one shift forced me to become aware of my emotions, and to identify where I was reacting irrationally in situations that I had no control over.

If you take this challenge for even one week, I promise you'll see your life from a different perspective. Once you begin to feel good about yourself and your life there's no longer any room for resentment, regret, rage – or revenge for that matter. Acknowledge them. Thank them for the reminder, and be done with them. It's not a good idea to carry around unnecessary toxic emotions that steal moments of goodness from us. They will take over if you allow them to.

Questions to Ponder

- If I have regrets that have changed people's lives, what could I do now to mend those relationships?

- What action can I take to remove the regret from my life today?

- To whom do I owe an apology that I stubbornly refuse to admit?

- What is my biggest regret? And if I only had six months to live, how important is it for me to undo it if I still can?

List your regrets and then let them go.

List your resentments then let them go.

When rage starts to surface breathe deeply and ask yourself is it going to be worth it?

Ask yourself in each of these moments, will it matter in six months? A year? Five years? The answer is usually a resounding NO!

Fixing your regrets today is very important.

Letting go of resentment is vital.

Living a life without anger and rage or a need for revenge in it is singlehandedly the most important aspect of living a life that matters.

Where is the time for joy in any of these wasted emotions?

Follow the elimination diet.

THE ELIMINATION DIET:

"Remove anger, regret, resentment,
Guilt, blame, and worry.
Then watch your health, and life, improve."

–Charles F. Glassman

WEEK 7: THE PATH TO HEALTH

"Health is wealth"

-Karen Kane

Journal entry: I woke up today again with illness. I had a sore throat and a cough for the third time in three months. If stress is the reason then I completely understand. With all the different aspects of my life, it has been virtually impossible to shake it in my environment. Right now even the sound of a phone ringing or a text going off has my skin curling.

With less than six months to live you would think that nothing in the world would matter.

Real or not, I have to ask myself the million-dollar questions: What in this stressful environment is worth being ill for? Is arguing with the boss worth my dis-ease? Is proving myself right to anyone worth my inner peace?

What inside of me is blocking, even under these circumstances, the ability to watch as it all rolls quietly off my back and not shake my core existence? What if I decided to let everybody solve his or her own problems? No judgment, no fixing, just loving support and offering advice only when asked.

I was frustrated with the fact that even though I knew all this was destroying what little good health I was able to hang on to, I continued to put other's needs before my own. This led to nights of no sleep, endless to-do lists, and sucking it up every time I wanted to scream F____ YOU!

The real me – the friendly, easygoing spontaneous, charming, peaceful me, is buried under mountains of emails, bills, life problems, angry words, resentments, and all of this is self-inflicted.

I've become a fighter to stand up for what I believe in no matter what the consequence. Do not for a second believe that I don't think this sore throat has everything to do with truly finding my voice through this process.

We have to be true to ourselves, otherwise this people-pleasing crap begins to cover our spirit like a layer of yuck clinging to our skin. Energetically, it will begin to attack every cell in our body, weakening us and making us ill. People who live their life without the stress of making sure everybody else is happy, are happy people themselves, and good health is the beautiful by-product. It shows. Their energy is felt deep inside like a warm glow. They usually light up a room when they walk in. As Joel Osteen reminds us, "When you're tempted to be upset, ask yourself, 'Is this worth giving up my joy?'"

Today this is what I want to feel. I want all this dis-ease, worry, and fake stature to leave me forever. I want to smile more and worry less. I have a Facebook friend who is one of the most positive loving people I know. Each day she's grateful for her family and she sends them loving posts. I often read her posts and wonder how she remains in such a positive state that I can feel her energy from afar. After all, she has problems too. When we're inspired by others it is such a gift. Often we have no idea how we can inspire others with a simple word of praise and joy. Ruth E. Renkel, a German author states the obvious when she writes, "You live longer once you realize that anytime spent being unhappy is wasted."

Being happy is our responsibility. Well-being breeds happiness. I'm at my happiest when I feel good physically and emotionally. In order for this to be my ongoing reality, I must eliminate the negative, draining aspects of my life. Mandy Hale, author of The Single Woman's Sassy Survival Guide writes, "It's not selfish to love yourself, take care of yourself, and to make your happiness a priority. It's necessary." When all else fails, my number one piece of advice is to go to the beach. I have no doubt that it will raise your spirit, and increase your health and happiness. There is nothing like beach mentality to increase your health. A life–long friend Florence shared her story called "Jail Break" with me which documents her journey to health through her choice to leave a job she loved but that was killing her physically.

Jail Break

Some people appear to be born free. They know what they want to be when they grow up. What they like. What they don't. They have singular focus and always seem to be moving in the right direction.

I am not one of them.

The closest I ever got to authentically self-determined career aspirations was imagining myself as a flight attendant when I was a little girl. It sounded fabulous. The outfits. The travel. Then I grew up, relatively speaking, and topped the charts at a whopping 5'2", missing the mandated height requirements of the time by just a smidgen. Then I got on a plane. I have one word. Dramamine.

After recovering from my dashed dream of becoming Flight Attendant Barbie, instead of making emotionally smart decisions about my professional life, I followed the path of least resistance. This may sound strange coming from someone with an advanced degree and a quarter century in academe, but it's true nonetheless. For over 25 years I made myself a prisoner of ease, convenience, security, and not rocking the boat. It was a winning formula, until it wasn't. Then I lost it. Full-blown mid-life crisis kind of lost it.

Prior to losing it, however, it was surprisingly simple to fall into the trap of letting my career run my life. All my goals were set for me by the system. There was little emotional work to do except to follow the ready-made path, ride out the bumps, and proceed as directed to each new milepost. The intellectual work was enjoyable. I loved it. The fact that the goals laid out for me were extrinsic and foreign to who I was at the time didn't slow me down a bit. In fact, I barely noticed. I had always been a "good girl". Following directions was easy.

I was successful. I earned my terminal degree, got a tenure-track job, left it, got another tenure-track job, did what I was told, got tenure, and became department head. All the while, I was dying a slow death. I had become the academic equivalent of Willy Loman, going to work every day in a self-constructed straight jacket. It is important to point out that it wasn't a "bad" job. In fact, I had a good job, with wonderful colleagues, in a very nice place. My malaise was never about other people or the blame game. My problem was how the career hung on me. It was like itchy clothes, too tight pants, or a low-cut, leopard print sweater. On someone else the ensemble would have been just right, but on me it was totally wrong. I felt like a fraud, an outsider, an outlier, and I wasn't emotionally adept enough to make the alterations necessary for a good fit.

And so it went. I ignored every sign that it might be time to leave. I cried on my way to work every day. I fantasized about driving by my turnoff, getting on the highway, and never looking back. The end of Thelma and Louise looked more and more appealing. Yep. I contemplated driving my cherry red Ford Ranger over the edge of the Grand Canyon. You know you're in trouble when you can't decide between quitting your job and driving your truck over a cliff, no matter how glamorous the latter looks on celluloid. I chuckle at the dichotomy all these years later: Should I resign or end it all? Deep down I always knew the Grand Canyon scenario was never really a viable choice. But it lay there in the background, teasing me with yet another easy way out. I was in trouble, big, messy, emotional trouble.

But, how do you leave a professional position you've worked years to attain? How do you give up security? I have to admit, I'm not sure, even now, that I would have been strong enough to make a break for it under my own steam. I was sick and depressed and I knew it, but I didn't have the wherewithal to make a move on my own. Fortunately, just the right help came from our university president, at just the right time. The institution was experiencing a budget crunch so he cancelled salary negotiations and did not issue contracts at the end of the school year. The scenario left the door open just wide enough for me to walk through and take a look around because it was summer and I did not have a signed contract for the upcoming academic year. I realize now it wasn't about the university issuing me a guarantee of continued employment. That was a given. I had tenure and I'd had a stellar year, at least on paper.

The real issue was that I am loyal to a fault. If I make a promise, I follow through. But this time was different. With no signed contract in hand, I had not promised to return for the coming year and so was free to begin the process of imagining a different path. I had no idea what it looked like or where it led. None whatsoever. I'd spent the entirety of my adult life working at one thing. I wasn't crafty or creative in any marketable way. I was so buried in my job that I could barely catch a glimpse of what I might like to do outside of it, except spend time with my family, hike, read, ski, and kayak. I didn't really see a viable career path for myself in any of those things. But, with the door slightly ajar, a crack began to appear in my professional façade. I began to believe that something else might be possible.

Before considering all the possibilities, however, I threw up. A lot. The mid-summer day my contract finally arrived I became so violently ill that even I could not ignore the signs. I talked with my husband and son. We came to the conclusion that the finances of my impending unemployment would not sink our ship. And so, I was free. For perhaps the first time in my life I didn't play it safe. I jumped into the unknown. Instead of signing on the dotted line, I resigned. Then I slept. Well, not at first. But pretty soon thereafter I began to sleep through the night, my lifelong battle with insomnia fading into the background. Then, I started melting. Literally. I woke up one morning and weighed less than the day before. No diet, just a little peace, and sleep; lots and lots of sleep. OK. I also gave up the huge latte and frosted scone I picked up every morning on my way to work, because there was no work.

The old me would have been petrified by the prospect of no job, no latte, and no scone. The old me would have settled for the first easy, familiar thing that came along. But I wasn't the old me anymore. Once I summoned up the courage to resign, something fundamentally shifted in me and I knew I could never go back to my self-made prison. Instead of telling myself scary stories based on past events that no longer mattered, I spent more time with my family. I hiked more with the dog. I gave myself the gift of time to figure out what I really wanted to do. After a lifetime of wearing masks to make myself fit into other people's schema, that was not such an easy thing.

So, I wrote. And wrote some more. I thought a lot and regained a sense of myself separate from my career. I lost a few old friends. I found some new ones. I made a radical decision to choose a path completely different from academe and in the process discovered that I have an innate ability to learn all sorts of new things, even stuff that baffled me in my youth. Who knew? I certainly didn't.

But now I do. And that makes all the difference in the world.

4 December 2015
Jail Break
An original, previously unpublished essay by: Florence Moorhead-Rosenberg

Questions to Ponder

- If I had to make a choice between money and health what would be more important?

- If I can't take care of myself, who will take care of me?

- What steps do I have in place to take care of myself, or my family in the event of illness?

- Do I have a long-term health plan? (Because if I keep going at this rate I'll surely need it).

- When I do not stop long enough to tame the madness around me, what is it doing to my body inside?

- Where do I feel the most discomfort in my body during stressful times?

- What everyday changes can I make to have health as the number one priority in my life?

- Am I eating to be healthy?

- How bad do I want to feel? (Do I like the drama?)

- How good do I want to feel?

This is a no-brainer. Without my health, I have nothing and I have no one. Health is the #1 priority, so take care of yourself first and everything else will follow. Health is wealth.

WEEK 8: THE TRUTH (LIVE YOUR AUTHENTIC SELF)

"Facts do not cease to exist because they are ignored."

-Aldous Huxley, Complete Essays 2, 1926-29

There are many, many kinds of lies. Small ones. Big ones. Fat ones. Skinny ones. Fabricated, outlandish ones. Two faced ones. Those you force yourself to believe. Justified ones. Innocent ones (if that's possible), and those one of a kind life-changing ones.

We're all guilty of telling a small lie when people ask us, "How are you?" Our typical response is "fine." Alternatively, the one over used question on everybody's lips, "What's wrong?" The answer is always, "Nothing." Rarely do we say back, "I'm angry." "I'm frustrated and hurt," or "I'm feeling ecstatic, sexy, joyous, and delighted." What if we spoke the truth every time?

Most of the time these answers protect our exposure, and keep our authentic self-hidden from those closest to us. Those words become a mechanism to avoid conflict or bring up controversial issues. They also eat away at our true self and cloud our happiness. My favorite author, life coach and mentor, Nancy Levin, author of *Jump, AND YOUR LIFE WILL APPEAR©,* said, "When you don't tell the truth to yourself, the truth comes out sideways."

If you've ever bumbled through a lie, you will totally get this. Usually in the midst of a lie, the words don't add up and something always feels off. I know for me personally I have the inability to keep a straight face, avoiding eye contact, and adding to the hidden truths within.

Honoring our truth means always telling the truth and this isn't always the simplest thing to do. We justify our untruths by feeling that we're protecting people or ourselves from a harsh reaction. Spiritual speaker and author Carolyn Myss said, *"Exposure to the truth changes your life, period. Whether that truth is a revelation about personal honesty and integrity or a divine revelation that reorganizes your place in the universe. This is why most people run from truth rather than towards it."*

One night I told a *little white lie*. It was my birthday and I had my boyfriend's phone in my purse along with my own. I snuck to the bathroom and began a text to one of my children. I lifted my boyfriend's phone out first and set it on the stall counter. Then I left the stall, leaving it there. A panicked three minutes later, I dashed back to the spot and the phone had gone. "Why did you have my phone?" he asked. Instead of saying that I took it out to make a call, I decided to tell a little white lie. "Um, it started to ring so I took it out and must have put on the stall shelf." The truth was I didn't think about his phone, only my own, and for some reason I couldn't own up to that.

This one lie led to a night of GPS-ing miles down the road following the phone sensor as it moved across town. It also involved frantic calls to my provider and credit card companies for the online shopping accounts and a missed birthday dinner. He lost pictures of his daughter and pictures of us together, and it clearly dampened the night. Would things have gone differently if I hadn't told a lie? It's likely. At any rate it proves the theory that lies have ripple effects that can ultimately be seismic.

It certainly isn't always easy to tell the truth. One of the quotes I had on my list of "house rules" when my children were growing up read, "Tell the microscopic truth." Yet through this journey I had to admit that I haven't always been an honest person with other people or myself. I would lie about something that meant nothing to anyone but me. There's always a little piece of ourselves that we keep hidden from others, yet the truth always inevitably rises to the top.

I wanted to get Botox and I didn't want anyone to know. I felt a little shame, a little vain, and a little insecure about my aging face. My significant other called me as I was sitting at the Botox appointment and he asked where I was. *"Um, um, I'm at Costco." Ok, well down the street a little. Ok, well actually I'm ten miles away, but that's close, right?*

I knew he could find me on an app, yet I chose to lie anyway. He said rather righteously, "But your phone says otherwise?" It was too late, and it led to a lot of explaining about why I'd lied in the first place. I of course turned the whole thing around to make it his fault, as we often do when we're on the defensive. Then I relayed the story to my friends who rallied around me for validation. It ended up that *everybody knew I had gotten Botox*, and now so does the rest of the world.

My moment of privacy was gone forever. That's where I gained the most wisdom on this subject. It occurred to me that if I have to lie to anybody and most importantly to myself, what's the purpose of being here. What's my purpose if I can't show up authentically?

My lying wasn't his fault; it was my lack of faith in the process of honesty. My lack of faith in myself as a person with personal wants needs and desires. I lacked believing in myself enough to know I'm worthy of whatever I choose to give to myself to feel better.

I lacked the forethought that I'm in charge of my life. I lacked the ability to trust who I am, Botox or no Botox. I lacked the trust in him loving me no matter what I look like. I lacked the capacity to trust.

In that moment I realized that if I didn't get real, I wasn't living the full potential of my soul.

It became clear to me that I want to show up to everyone exactly how I am in every minute of every day. I decided to walk the talk, and with my theoretical idea of having only six months to live, I knew that quite possibly everybody will know pretty much everything about me in the end anyway. I heard this little voice inside me yelling, *"Stop it, just stop it. Be yourself and start living your life."* I decided to tell the truth to everybody in every instance for two weeks. No matter what somebody asked me I would answer honestly.

There were many times when I wished I'd held my tongue because sometimes the truth hurts, but this challenge was life changing.

What kept me going was an old saying I've kept dear to my heart throughout my entire life: "The truth hurts for a minute, but a lie lasts forever." This is so true. The truth telling process requires conscious thought in almost every instance. Every word that comes out of your mouth represents truth, and every action supports that truth, setting you in alignment with your truth. You get to be you and be accountable to only you and your actions. It's the freest I've ever felt. Free, alive, worthy, and clean.

Telling the truth leaves little scrambling for words and it feels uncontaminated.

The art of always telling the truth can set you on a path to getting real. I called people out when my feelings were hurt and let them know; a truth I often kept hidden to spare their discomfort in spite of my own. I said no when I meant no (when I usually would have said yes because of the people-pleaser in me). I stopped explaining myself or defending my actions, and then something magical happened. As a result, I've gotten to know myself. I have no other mission in my day other than to be me. Authentically.

The biggest lies have the biggest effects. The life changing lies are catastrophic and sometimes beyond repair. I ordered a new phone, but how do you order a new friend after you were two-faced, or a new spouse after infidelity? How do you replace the child indoctrinated by one vindictive parent who allows them to grow up not knowing one true fact about their family or identity?

Further, if you end up being the recipient of another person's lie, you suddenly question everything you ever believed. And I know from my own experience that I spent endless hours trying to figure out why people didn't trust me enough to show up 100 percent authentically.

If we want to truly live and be present in each day, we can't afford to lie. We can let our truth be known and let life unfold, draping us with the knowledge that we're right where we're supposed to be. Once we've felt that clean feeling of showing up authentically and feel the weight off our back by simply telling the truth, we won't want to reignite the heavy feeling of a lie.

To continue lying to anyone about anything is cheating every single person a chance to love us authentically. When we lie it's like having a 50 lb. weight on our shoulders. When we lie and come clean, it feels as if someone took a power washer and cleansed your soul. If I can't be me and tell the microscopic truth, how will I ever truly know who am I? What's the purpose of one more day let alone six more months?

This month I'm trying to clean all this up. I want to die clean. This journey is about telling the truth to me about me. It's about cleaning up my past actions, owning my current and future actions, and telling people I'm sorry.

Questions to Ponder

- What untruths are hiding out there to be uncovered after I'm gone?

- Whom will they hurt?

- Who deserves to hear the truth from me now?

- Write down that truth and do not leave out any details.

- What event in your life do you feel has been more important to cover up then open up?

- Why?

- What stops me from telling the truth and showing up exactly as I am?

- What is my fear?

What could possibly be better than feeling the weight of dishonesty lifted off your spirit? I value my authenticity way more than I value covering myself up. It doesn't serve anyone to lie to anyone. I almost laugh now at the thought of lying. It takes far too much energy, way, too much to remember, and it's simply never worth it. As my grandmother always said, "Everything comes out in the wash." I just prefer to be the one airing the laundry from now on. Lesson learned.

There are few things in life so beautiful they hurt; swimming in the ocean when it rains, reading alone in empty libraries, the sea of stars that appear when you're miles away from neon lights of the city, bars after 2am, walking in the wilderness, all the phases of the moon, the things we do not know yet about the universe, and you."

-Beau Taplin via afadthatlastsforever

MONTH 3

WEEK 9: THE DRAMA DETACHMENT

"When I loved myself enough, I began leaving whatever wasn't healthy. This meant people, jobs, my own beliefs and habits, anything that kept me small. My judgment called it disloyal. Now I see it as self-loving."

-Kim McMillen

I do not have to react. How I never knew that until now is beyond me.

The realization that I don't have to erupt with a spontaneous combustion every time something happens that isn't "perfect" was the greatest gift. Being able to take a deep breath and go inside to find that place of calm instead of responding from your dark side will bring so much peace into your life.

Yet we are triggered on a daily basis. *We cannot go on like this.* Reacting to every little thing as if it is the end of the world will only help you to die a slow painful death that will last for years! You forgot to pay the phone bill. The towels sat in the dryer wet. The dog peed on the floor. Your boss slammed his door. Your child broke a vase. As you read you are probably thinking, "Um, this isn't end of the world stuff," but you know that at some time in your life you've reacted to a similar event with more drama than was necessary.

The only end of the world is when you die. And even then it's only the end of this world. So looking at the bigger picture, I can't find one good reason to keep myself engulfed in drama. When someone comes at me about how I've ruined their day because of something I didn't do for them, I don't buy into the drama anymore. When somebody starts screaming at me, I run. I'm past trying to change the way something goes by ranting about it or hearing someone else ranting about it. That never changes anything. I can honestly say that unless I was unquestionably right about something, I've never had the power to change the drama through ranting.

My day started with coffee all over the counter. This happens, often. Either the coffee maker isn't clean enough or it's broken. I cringe inside when this one silly thing happens.

Then began a typical *OMG why* rant. I got in the car and drove straight to Starbucks. "Two coffees please," I said, and I was back home in five minutes. Here is your coffee. But no, it was too late for the others in my life. The day was ruined. Normally, it ruining anyone else's day would ruin my day too. I love my family, but I refuse to buy into the drama anymore. Things like coffee spilt on a counter do not matter when you have only six months to live. What matters is that in spite of the mess, you continue to have a blissful day. You still meet the day with gratitude and keep looking to find the good. It's the way of the peaceful warrior.

On most of those coffee spilled days, I then proceeded to the drama capitol of the world, which was my office, where drama after drama tested me all day. I couldn't believe that I remained unaffected. Then it hit me that I may have crossed the finish line on this one.

Today I discovered the powerful reality that I don't have to react to anything. I don't have to let anyone else's mood or issues or power trips, or disappointments or idiosyncrasies affect ME. I know on an organic level that life is much too short to let little upsets ruin a good day, a good evening, or a good month.

Eleven hours later, I'm on a hammock in 85 degree weather doing my favorite thing after a long work day. Nothing. And listening to my favorite reminder song "Just Breathe" by Anna Nalick.

Reaction is key. I've learned how important it is to my well-being to keep my cool.

Why do we thrive on drama? Why do we surround ourselves with people who thrive on drama? We all know that someone; the one you're almost afraid to call because their energy overtakes you. Sometimes you even buy into it.

We can always count on one little thing to turn into a big thing. One person to react bigger than we think is appropriate, which for me usually brings a huge feeling of overwhelm. Besides death, nothing is debilitating enough that you can't find a solution that lessens the dramatic "my life is ending" feeling. The solution is to stop reacting without taking a breath first. Close your mouth for long enough to listen to your heart and ask yourself one simple question: Will this matter in six months?

I learned a valuable lesson through drama detachment. The day I lost my job, I felt I had been thrown to the curb, discarded, betrayed, and violated after enduring a toxic situation for months. And I felt I deserved none of it.

I lived and breathed, "What happened" for months on end to anyone who would listen, and even those who would not or didn't want to. Every time I saw my one faithful "Jerry McGuire moment" friend who was there when it all went down I'd relive the story over and over.

I could rationalize, justify, defend myself, and she would listen and support my every word with real concern. Then one day while we were rehashing the story, she said ever so politely, "When I had a similar situation in my past, I remember it was all I could talk about until I realized people were tired of hearing it. They had moved on and I hadn't."

Like a shot in my arm, I understood. It was still going on for me because I was keeping it going through the telling of the story. The pain was still inside me because I wouldn't let it go. I couldn't detach and see the situation objectively. I couldn't see past my piece of the situation to understand that everybody else had his or her own version.

The problem was, I had no idea how to stop talking about it. It was consuming me.

We can create how dramatic something is in our lives. Our thoughts can make it bigger than its intended life span. Our need to justify our part has us ranting and raving like a lunatic when the energy spent to do that is sometimes unhealthier for us than what may have happened.

What if we looked at every drama trauma in our lives as a blessing? Like a beam of light to take us on a different path. What if, because I had to clean up the coffee, I avoided a car accident? What if, I reacted and started yelling at someone and they had a heart attack and died?

What if?

What if we could believe that we're always protected by a greater power than our silly little story of woe? What if every crisis could be averted, with a deep understanding that everything is exactly as it's supposed to be? What if we shared a simple knowing that inner peace is always right in front of us? Let's face it, in almost all circumstances when you ask, 'Will this matter in six months?' it's almost always a no. And if it will, ask, 'Will it matter in a year? Or five years?' It's usually a resounding hell no!

How many times has something happened to you that you thought, "I don't know how I'm going to get through this." Yet you do?

When we stop talking about something, it miraculously goes away and opens up our thought channels to create and live a life free from drama. Inspirational speaker Esther Hicks' number one advice for being happy is to "just shut up about things that do not bring happy thoughts!" It makes so much sense when you think about it.

We are responsible for having drama in our life.

Learning to detach is quite simple and I've found an effective way that works:

First, when drama comes up, don't be afraid to confront it in the moment. Trust the flow of your feelings. By trusting the flow, you stay in the flow. When things happen that cause you to doubt everything and you're ready to throw your hands in the air and shut it all down, throw them up and know it's just life. In other words, when you feel yourself spiraling into drama zone, surrender to the outcome. Surrender is not giving up, it's giving it up to a power much higher than us. Surrender is faith. Once you detach from the outcome, and starve the drama, you open the door to all things good.

If it is something I can't let go, I furiously type an imaginary text message or email about it. I imagine the worst as I'm writing. I blame everybody, I play the victim one last time, and then I delete it. Then every time a thought comes into my head about it, I ask myself how the weather is? I say to myself, "Isn't the sky a pretty blue?" Whenever anyone brings it up, I change the subject deliberately. I remind myself that I'm right where I'm supposed to be in this moment. This could go on once an hour or more, but the point is I'm not focusing on the drama unless it's in front of me in the moment.

Some people call this denial and not "dealing," and I'm not saying it's not denial, I'm just saying that it works. To be happy you have to cut out the drama and the situations or people that bring it to you, including your thoughts about it.

I went to counseling for two years, and God bless my dear therapist who listened and guided me through this painful time. Yet he ultimatley realized that no progress was made in getting me to let go of the story of woe I was telling. He kindly explained to me that it was time to stop re-hashing the story- over and over again. When I stopped telling the story and the painful memories subsided, the pain miraculously disappeared. There's always going to be residue from these painful life-changing traumas but they don't need to run your days anymore. Use the drama to be fierce about what's next. Remember the event but forget the effect it had on you. Keep focused on what's good because what I know for sure is that after every big drama trauma, something good is coming right around the corner.

Tonight, as I escape into the land of my DVR where I quietly watch a dramatic teeth-clenching show with lots of drama and trauma, I remember I get all the drama I'll ever need from a television show, thank you!

Questions to Ponder

- If I only have six months to live, is there anything out there from a spilled cup of coffee to a car cutting me off, to a bill I'm unable to pay, to a phone call I don't want to answer, to a person I don't want to interact with…Is there anything more important than my sanity and my daily dose of peace?

- What drama or story are you holding on to that is holding you back from living in the present today?

- What changes can you make to lessen the drama in your life?

- At work:

- At home:

- In relationships:

- Who brings drama into your life?

- What would you tell them about how it is affecting you if you could?

Write out or tell someone the most dramatic version of "your story." Let everyone in it have a piece and then burn it. Be done with it. Let it go.

WEEK 10: TODAY

"We all have two lives. The second one starts when we realize we only have one."

–Tom Hiddleston

Journal Entry:

"If you're not living each day of your life as if it was your last, you're wasting time…"

    This was my profound thought last night as I raced across the lake detoxing from my week at work. I sat and looked at the water sparkling, the boaters laughing, the sun shining, and I thought that even after the miserable Friday workday- life at this very moment is good. Happiness is in the air, people are smiling, couples are hugging, kids are jumping in and out of the water. I often forget how good life is in the midst of my uncomfortable settings. I'm sucked into the negativity of others as if I never had a thought that was my own. Then I think, if this is my last day, I want to feel this beauty. I won't waste this moment worrying about tomorrow. Note to self: it's wasted energy and has toxic results on your psyche. Let's just say this is my last day on earth and I'm out on a boat with the man I love and I feel zero self-consciousness (even if I have a stomach roll in the bikini I shouldn't be wearing). And let's just say I feel sexy enough and confident enough because I know that this is when I feel the best. And let's just say that the things that happened to me to present the need for this detox have vanished from my thoughts. And let's just say that I'm sitting in this moment breathing in the goodness, breathing in the happiness and energy of all these local vacationing souls. What a waste of my life and time if I were to entertain any thought or worry about tomorrow instead of allowing all this heaven on earth to absorb me. My body craves the feeling of clean, and I'm not talking about my house. I'm talking about that clean 'nothing toxic in my environment' feeling, and no thoughts, people or behaviors that feed it. This is the feeling that I crave and that sets the tone for blissful days.

What does tomorrow mean?

I recently posted an eye-opening definition I found on Facebook, "Tomorrow" (noun) a mystical land where 99% of all human productivity, motivation and achievement is stored." Author unknown.

When I was in my twenties and thirties I barely had time to think about what I wanted "tomorrow" to look like. Raising children and working three jobs left little time to ponder the future. What it did do though was only allow me to honor the day in front of me. I just didn't know it at the time. It took everything to get one day planned out in front of me with three kids and a grandchild living with me.

A "Typical Today": I have to drop off three kids, get to the eye doctor, and call the phone company. Make an appointment. Grocery shop. Pay bills. Go to bank. Cheer practice. Pick up child two from work. The list was endless on some days and then if anything didn't get done, then and only then did it get put off until tomorrow.

When my day changed to kids driving themselves, and making life decisions that didn't include me, I started to live in the future, planning all the things I was going to do. *When I have enough money. When I retire. When I get a day off.* We start to see a future that we held back for so long out there in visible proximity with delight, and just about then something unexpected crashes into your life to change your path. You may meet someone unexpectedly. You may be invited on a vacation that changes your entire year. You may get a medical prognosis forcing you to look at your life in a different way. You may start looking at your life as if it was wasted away at a dead end job, and therefore you feel unfulfilled.

You then start listening to an inner voice telling you there's something more and you seek it out with a silent vengeance. However, we can unknowingly keep that calling out there because we're too afraid to jump into the unknown and live our true purpose. We don't have enough money yet. We have a job to do, bills to pay, and sometimes we don't even trust ourselves enough to surrender and take a chance. The mentality I needed to change this was by taking those chances every day, with the observation that if I don't go for it today, it might be my last chance.

Each day I wake up and *only* tackle what is in front of me. This took some real adjustments because the 'fly by the seat of my pants' gypsy soul, although a lot of fun, hindered my motivation. I thought, "How can I plan for a future if I'm supposed to only live "today" in the moment?" It started to annoy me that nothing was getting done. Only little projects here and there. A book to finish, a business to create, family stuff, friendship stuff, life decisions, and then it hit me.

Living in today is a feeling. I live each moment as if it is my last because *it could be.* I live each day as if it is all I have *because it is all I have.* When I start my day with gratitude because I'm blessed with one more day to see the sun come up, I'm living in today. When I end each day with no regrets, no resentment for anyone or anything, and I go to sleep conscious that every night when I close my eyes I'm putting faith in the fact that I'll wake up again, I'm living in today. Nothing is more freeing for your mind. Just breathe in today. Stop right this second, look around you, and pinch yourself. You are living in today.

I still make lists and together with my life-coach I created a weekly calendar of "Cathslife" just to keep me on track with some semblance of balanced life. I never, however, think that what I wrote down for tomorrow won't be altered. Nine times out of ten it does get altered.

This is why we can only truly acknowledge today. Today is where things happen. Yesterday cannot and will not ever be changeable. Tomorrow is 100 percent mystical, so although this is going to sound super cliché, ALL WE HAVE IS TODAY. We have no idea almost hour to hour what is going to change. How one phone call will change your life. How one encounter with a single person can turn your world upside down in an instant. We only have today to say I love you. Today to say I'm sorry. Today to say yes. Today to say no. Today to make that important call. Today to reach out to the person on our mind. Today to honor our sacred feelings. Today to do something kind. Today to say thank you. Today- today- today.

I couldn't get away from the thoughts that were forcing me to stop living as if the answer is in my tomorrow, and stop beating myself up about what happened yesterday, or last week, or last month, or ten years ago. In a recent call with my life coach I was working on letting things go, and I said, "Oh my God, it has been sixteen years and I'm still carrying this." She said ever so quietly, whispering in a way I'd never forget, *"Exactly."*

Lesson #182 – Today is all I have.

WEEK 11: ONE DAY IN AMERICA

"What separates us from the animals, what separates us from the chaos, is our ability to mourn people we've never met."

-David Lethian

During one simple month of this journey, death began to surround me. I found out a friend had died. He was one of the happiest men I knew: in love with his wife, a devoted father and son, a brother and an uncle. He was at the top of his game at work and he had just purchased his dream home. Due to a random act of nature he died within fifteen minutes. I was crushed when I heard the news. I had to live with the realization that even though I'd been writing about this process; death was no easier to swallow for me.

I would miss him and I realized how much he had done for my family. Two days before, I was driving by his workplace and I had the thought to stop in and say hello, but I didn't. I had no idea how affected I would be, or how angry I would be at the universe for this. It simply wasn't fair. I'd never experienced anyone in as much grief as his wife at his funeral.

I had this period of letting go and knowing that I wasn't in control of anything, even death. I found myself questioning the universe. Could it be that we aren't in control? Period? That when it's our time to go, we will just - go?

Shortly following that, I received the morning phone call while driving to my grandmothers 105th birthday party that no one wants to get. It starts with, "I have some bad news." As I heard the news, and absorbed the announcement of a very tragic car accident killing someone very close, I was speechless for more than a minute. It was as if the entire universe had stopped spinning for a moment and I drove in an orbited state for over a mile.

Then I turned on Facebook and saw that Dr. Wayne Dyer had died. I had recently seen him lecture and thought for sure he was immortal. It always comforted me to hear him say "You are an infinite spiritual being having a temporary human experience." His death shook me and the spiritual world, but I have no doubt that he is still spreading his wisdom around the world.

If you've ever woken up in the morning and turned on the news, you'll notice a little ticker tape that runs across the bottom of your screen. *A car crash killed three people...a plane crashed with 54 people on board...no survivors...an unknown assailant targeted a shopping mall...1 killed 3 injured in a 7 car accident...2 boaters missing at sea...*

Read it some time. This usually represents just one day, yet this stuff happens 365 days a year several times a day, streamed from over 50 national television news stations in the country.

Esther Hicks, my favorite inspirational speaker, has been known to preach rather loudly that watching the news is a surefire way to ruin the excitement of life and kill all remnants of joy. I tend to agree. After a year and half of watching the news and then six months of not, I felt quiet inside.

It became so clear to me during this time that life was very unpredictable and the idea of choosing our destiny date with death was fascinating to me. In the book Dying to be Me, Anita Moorjani, a gentle woman who died from advanced stage 4 cancer and chose to come back rather than pass to the other realm, will convince you about her experience of going to the other side. She describes her experience there as the most beautiful brilliance of light and a blissful feeling of unconditional love and connectedness with every single creature on the planet. She also iterates that she had a choice to stay or go and the difficulty she had choosing to come back into a sickened body. She had a knowing that if she chose to come back to life, "her body would heal rapidly and they wouldn't be able to find a trace of the cancer." And in weeks, it turns out that she was completely cancer free.

I spent years living in fear of death.

I wouldn't fly in an airplane because my best friend's mom, who was more than a mother to me, died in a plane crash when I was twenty. She had followed her heart to be with the man she loved, went off on a yearlong journey and lost her life. I was watching the news when I saw that a plane out of New Zealand had struck the side of a mountain in Iceland and I froze. I knew. Within seconds I received the call. It was about six years ago that I finally started to fly again.

I was fifteen years old when I had my first face to face with death. I watched in horror as a young girl was thrown out of the back of a truck full of friends, riding on a warm summer night to a local hang. Trails of cars behind, all going to the same place, and then the truck lost control around a turn and bodies flew out. I was petrified to ride with anyone after that, and I never again got in the back of a truck to drive anywhere.

The more I started to investigate this, the more evidence there seemed to be that these events weren't always random. I don't know this for sure, and quite possibly I never will, but I do know that we never know where one day will take us, even with diagnoses of six months to live because I've witnessed and listened to people who have evaded death under the most extreme, unimaginable, illogical circumstances. A high school friend shares his brush with the other side with us.

Tony's Trip to The Other Side and Back

In the early morning of December 9th 2011, just after midnight, I received a phone call from Kathy, my pre-transplant coordinator. I had been ill with cirrhosis of the liver and suffering from encephalopathy, a problem when ammonia instead of oxygen enters the brain. I was unable to do most day to day things. I was awaiting this call with much trepidation for a while and now it was here.

I was told that they had a match for my liver and needed me in CPMC Hospital on Buchannan St in San Francisco in 4 hours for a liver transplant. I called my brother Tim who picked me up and got me to the hospital around 1 am. After filling out paperwork, I was put into a room to prep for the operation. It was about this time that I have lost memory.

Aside for a few, brief moments of being aware of my surroundings, I was unconscious until the day before Christmas.

During this "unconscious" state of being, there was a myriad of what I perceived were dreams that I had. However, one of these dreams seemed more real than any dream that I have ever had.

I found myself in the family room of the house in which I grew up. I was talking with my Dad and my brother Tom. It seemed just like a normal evening I'd had many times growing up, chatting with my family. The only difference is that my Father and Tom had been dead for years. As they got up to leave, I followed. Tom went out, then Dad put his hand on my chest and said, "No". He turned through the door and closed it on me. I went out the other door and then I heard other family members talking. I opened my eyes and saw my very much alive brothers Tim and Terry. I think that I smiled, then went back to sleep. One thing was abundantly clear to me when I awoke: It was not my time to die.

I think of that moment of thought often, and it has changed me. Sometimes I have an overwhelming feeling of joy for being given a second chance. An indescribable feeling that all is good. Unfortunately, I occasionally have a feeling of survivor-guilt. Why am I alive and someone unknown to me is not? Fortunately, the simple joy of being alive takes over, and it is the most overwhelmingly feeling of peace.

I know that I am no better than anyone else, but also no worse. I try now to live each day to the fullest with knowledge that my actions really do matter to others. We are not alone. Actually, I have gained the wisdom through this experience that we are all connected in life, and in death. I now see the wonders of life through peoples smiles and laughter, especially in children. It warms my heart so much that often I get teary-eyed at the simplest moments in life. Being alive and having a chance to help others, even if that means just to give a needed smile, means everything to me! I enjoy being alive and making others smile, and my joy is infectious. Maybe I was sent back through that life door to teach people that life is made up of joyous moments and that now is the time to appreciate them.

Tony Bosque

So when is our time to go? I'd always believed that it was predestined, but this was becoming more than "it's your time to go." This became about the possibility that we have a choice. Anita Moorjani also wrote that the moment she chose to come back it was "understood that my body is only a reflection of my internal state and that all she had to do now was be herself." In other words, it all depends on how you feel. What emotions you let dominate.

I don't know when my time will come any more than you do. I do know that I've heard people say, "Oh I'm going to die from this, this or this." And sometimes they're even jovial about it, as if they picked it.

Watching and studying life events that came out of nowhere and seeing lives changed forever in their wake was too much to ignore. I wanted to know more about what these random events meant and I wanted to follow the dots that connect us in this world to try to put some rational to it.

I couldn't wrap my head around the undeniable circumstances that listening to one small voice in your head or changing a plan could alter the path of thousands or just one person in the same breath. One of my oldest and dearest friends Debra shared a story that haunted her for several years and I invited her to share it with us. I think it epitomizes the definition of following your callings from the other side.

Debra's Story: It was night-time, around 7pm. Dark. I was by myself driving to the mall to do shopping. From my house to the mall it's a ten minute drive. The road I was traveling wasn't a main road so there were no cars around.

All of a sudden, the most intense overwhelming energy of fear washed over me. It was so intense that it's hard to find the right words to describe it. The power of this energy of fear was so great that I literally felt I had no control of it. It was like a direct warning that I was about to be in a car accident. I could even perceive that the impact was going to be on my side of the car. It was such a strange unfamiliar feeling. All around me was darkness, and I could see no headlights anywhere, but I couldn't shake the thought that the energy was sending me a warning. I was so afraid that I pulled over on the side of the road. I turned off my radio and kept my car running. I sat there so incredibly frightened, I couldn't move. It was as if this powerful energy of fear completely filled my whole car. It was like the energy after an earthquake; an unexplainable force of sorts. I don't remember how long I sat there, but finally the energy of fear subsided. It felt strange, like coming out of a fog. I suddenly felt safe to drive, and brushed it off as anxiety. I started driving up the road when after a mile or so there had been terrible accident. I couldn't believe it! There were two cars, and I could see people running around them. I could see someone in one of the cars, and that car had been hit on the driver's side. It looked like a bad accident. I know that was the accident I would have been in. I couldn't believe my eyes and I was a nervous wreck. I knew that people were helping and so I drove past the accident and I didn't stop driving until I reached the mall. I was a mess. I parked and walked to the phone booth to call my husband (this was before cell phones). I remember breaking down in tears as I told him what had happened. I went back to the parking lot and sat in my car trying to get control of my emotional state and calm myself down so I could drive home. It took a while. I'll always remember that night, and I'll never ever forget that invisible energy of fear, the unexplainable power that forced me to pull over when there was nothing concrete to explain why I should. There's no question that it was a direct warning that I was about to be in a car accident. There was no other purpose but to protect me from getting in that accident. It was as if I was in another dimension, or what I believe to be a guardian angel. What other explanation can there be?

Debra Spilliotis

This one news story stopped me in my tracks. Reported in Glendale, California: a three-year-old child accidently fell out of a two-story window and survived. How she survived is what floored me. Below the window, a couple *just happened* to be moving in their new mattress and it was there to shield the fall at the exact precise moment needed to save the child's life. The serendipitous moment here is that one hour before; they had been stuck in an elevator for thirty minutes. If this hadn't had happened, THEY WOULDN'T HAVE BEEN IN THAT EXACT PLACE AT THAT EXACT TIME. This is proof that we're all exactly where we're supposed to be. Moments are all we have, so there's no need to worry about the future because it's going to unfold exactly as it's supposed to.

Is death just random or is it something we choose? Why does one family face unspeakable sadness with loss, while another jumps with joy by a saving grace? How could I continue living in a way that didn't support *who I really was*, with the awareness that each day brought a new set of circumstances that rather randomly took the life of a fellow human being? There absolutely was no time to be worried, fearful, unkind, ungrateful, mean, angry, resentful, rageful, bitter, dishonest, regretful or depressed, because I could be next! Or I could lose someone dear to me. It changed how I left people and the words I used to say goodbye.

When I was 14 years old my brother was accidently shot in the neck by his best friend. My father came and picked me up from a slumber party at six o'clock in the morning, and all I remembered was asking repeatedly, "Is he dead, is he dead?" My father replied in a quiet uncommon voice I never forgot, *"Not yet."* My brother recovered and is such a happy person today. My love for him is even greater because I remember almost losing him.

At the age of six, I remember a nun coming into my classroom to tell us that President Kennedy had been shot. One shot from one gun has altered the life of thousands and thousands of people to this day.

Years later I watched in horror when I was old enough to understand what had happened, the live shooting of his brother.

I remember the eerie shock and unexplainable grief I felt the day I learned about OJ Simpson's wife Nicole Brown and Ron Goldman, a very innocent man delivering glasses, who were found brutally murdered on a summer evening. She had been celebrating her daughter's dance recital, and ended her evening with a meal and a glass of wine, like we do all over the country every day. He, simply being kind.

This violent act changed America. It put a voice to spousal abuse, and reminded the world of a deep racial divide that had been buried for centuries. It introduced DNA, which has helped thousands of innocent people walk free for crimes they didn't commit, and convict people that may have gotten away. I still mourn for all of their families' every time they pop into the news or I pass the plethora of books in my library on the subject. Clearly, their death left a huge mark of change on many people's lives.

I remember the night Polly Klaus was kidnapped from her home while having a slumber party with children my own children's age, and eight weeks later her body was found thirty miles from my house. She was America's child. Everybody's little girl. Her picture hangs on my Christmas tree every year.

Polly Klaus's name went on to represent the face of the missing children that would follow in masses. Many things changed on how kidnappings were handled.

Sadly, she lost her life.

I remember so many different news stories that were earth-shattering, life stopping events that left us motionless at the thought of the change that had just occurred. Yet, there are stories every single day of people losing their lives in many different ways.

On September 11, 2001, terrorists flew planes into two buildings in the World Trade Center. In less than one hour 2,977 lives were lost. I'm confident that there's not one person in our world that doesn't remember where they were when this event occurred. It was frightening, tragic, and incomprehensible.

The synchronicities of this event and the accounts of the survivors really caught my attention. The people who were supposed to be there and somehow "weren't."

In almost every account that I've read about Sept 11, 2001, there's a resounding theme: *"All I remember is that it was a beautiful day."*

People laid off from their jobs just the day before, arrived later than usual, missing the bombings and discovering that their entire team of friends were gone.

I read accounts of people running back up the stairs to get their stuff, only to hear voices command out of nowhere, "LEAVE IT!" And they escaped unharmed.

One woman who never took breaks at work because she "didn't have time" was randomly invited for a smoke break twenty minutes before the planes hit, or she would have been sitting at her desk. Today she reminds her coworkers on a daily basis not to let their lives revolve around their jobs.

Life is serendipitous, so I have to believe that so is death. I find comfort in allowing my life to unfold in the intended path. I know that I can lose someone or someone can lose me in a moment. This one fact simplifies the entire process for me. *All we have is now.* Do not lose sight of the fact that just one day counts.

"When it is all finished, you will discover that it was never random"

-Author unknown

WEEK 12: EVERY ENCOUNTER MATTERS

"MY BARN HAVING BURNED TO THE GROUND I CAN NOW SEE THE MOON."

-Mizuta Masahide

This quote gifted to me from a friend, hangs in my office next to my desk as a constant reminder of the day my house and everything in it burned to the ground. It also reminds me that when this life-changing event happened, I had no insurance to pay for the destruction. The stark reality was that I had lost everything.

There I was at age forty standing in the ashes of my life after a series of life choices led me to this little cabin in the woods where I lived with my three children. It was the only thing left in a broken marriage and the only way to keep it was for me to move in and forfeit my then three-bedroom home rent in lieu of not letting go of the only asset I owned.

It had only one bedroom and a little camper trailer for my older son. A wood stove for heat and no television. We had dogs, cats, pigs, chickens, cows, horses, rabbits, dirt bikes, mud, dust and water, (a very valuable asset) that fed the house from a natural spring coming out of the side of the mountain into a pipe above the house. There were sixty-five acres of Redwoods, Pines, Douglas Firs, and trails upon trails of wonderland.

It was the saddest and the happiest time of my whole life.

I had made some huge life changing mistakes prior to this event. My marriage had ended two years earlier, and I was blaming him for all the mistakes of my life, when in reality I was experiencing my own midlife crisis and personal evolution, as I outgrew the vision of the perfect marriage. I opted for a fairytale turned nightmare that unexpectedly wreaked more chaos in my life than I could have imagined.

I spent the day at the Northern California coast town of Fort Bragg where "Mr. Fairytale" lived. It had been several months since our last encounter where I flipped him the bird as a parting gesture.

I think part of me was hoping to bump into him, and the other part of me had an unshakeable warning lurking in the back of my mind. I had received a psychic reading in the past week that continued to ring a truth in my ears I couldn't deny. She told me, *"If you don't run as fast as you can from this man you'll lose everything, including your children."*

I'd just finished the custody portion of my divorce where many stones were cast to paint me as an unfit Mother and it scared me to death to think I'd lose them over my bad choices.

I remember looking out at the ocean and retelling that story to my best friend, feeling and expressing that it felt so angry out there in the ocean that day and proclaiming that something in my life had to shift. She had been the rock by my side during what was one of the hardest times I'd ever experienced. We took a picture of ourselves, hair blowing, looks of bewilderment, smiles hiding the underneath layer of discomfort I could not shake, as if to document this life changing day. I'd come here to shed all the weight of the past months and start a new life. *This was the day* I was going to let go of the past and move forward. We had no idea at that time how much power could actually be behind that day's intention.

Then, that night I left the candle burning.

The same candle I was burning every night hoping for a miracle. Two candles on top of candles for weeks, until it had grown a third wick all on its own. Another girlfriend and I decided to go out for a drink on this memorable evening. We drove out of the driveway and I looked at her and said, *"Ooops, I left the candle burning, we should go back."* Then I had a second thought. *"No, it doesn't matter as it'll go out by itself."* I can't tell you how many times I've recanted this part of the story as a reminder of the inner knowing's we often fail to listen to.

When we arrived at the bar, I realized it had been a long time since I'd sat at a bar, let alone talked to another man. I sat down. *"Ok Cathy, you got this, just simple eye contact and a smile is all you need."* And I saw a man sitting at the bar with his head low.

I felt some odd pull to that suspense, and I couldn't put my finger on it. Scared to death I decided to spark a conversation with him. *"Thirty minutes,"* I thought. It turns out that I sat on that barstool for two hours longer than I should have, trying to convince a stranger that his wife and children were more than worth the drink in front of him. He was looking for a way to convince himself to check into rehab, wallowing in self-pity, blaming the world for his problems. Blaming everybody but himself.

There was no question by the end of that conversation that I was supposed to be there to give him a life-changing message. Now when I notice this happening, I think it's our guardian angels shining their wisdom right through us.

When I got home that night, I found twenty-five firefighters in my front yard as during those two hours my house had burned to the ground and I'd lost everything. And my friend lost her faithful dog, Mr. Head.

When I walked up to the fire fighter, he showed me where the hot spot was, and he handed me the only two possessions left – two statues of angels – the ones sitting right next to the candle monument, slightly burned. I still have them to this day.

On this single day I'd lost everything I owned. I can tell you from experience that the only thing I cared about was the photo albums. Three weeks later, ten photo albums were found in the ashes, all burned and 80 percent salvageable. I had lost nothing and gained just about everything a person "rising out of the ashes" needed to move on from an event like this.

I learned that every moment and every person that steps into your world has a gift for you. And you also have a gift for them. It might not be in a cute little package, but it's there to help you live and discover and unravel every layer of you. I've learned to embrace even the smallest of encounters or smiles. It gives me that sense of oneness. I've learned that when you don't take action to change your life when it isn't working, the universe will provide the change for you. My standard advice for friends in need of a change is *"Don't wait until they burn your house down,"* referring to the mystical law of the universe.

I found out later that the drunk man did indeed check into rehab the next day, and he's still with his wife today. For months I thought maybe I was supposed to be his angel that day. It took a bit longer for me to realize that he was mine. I never saw him again, but that single encounter that night, staying in that bar and making that choice to help him while my house was burning to the ground, changed my life in ways I could never have foreseen. It freed me of everything in my life that I was holding onto: a broken marriage, an even worse relationship after, and an old cabin that represented both of them. I went on to get a beautiful new home, meet many new people, and live a better life.

You can never underestimate the power of an hour.

We encounter new people every single day. On an airplane, in a bus or a taxi. In line at the bank. Ever had a silent nodding conversation with someone in heavy commute traffic that's going at turtle pace? There's an unspoken hello in most of these cases because you're all sitting there in the same boat waiting for the next moment in your lives to come. Life changing new encounters can happen every time we walk into a store or a restaurant, walk on a beach, go to an amusement park, and stand in long lines. The woman's restroom line at a concert is always alive with women wanting to chat. I actually met one of my best friends in a bathroom line. True story.

We have multiple opportunities to reach out and say hello to someone new every single day. We can exchange smiles with strangers and it could be a day changer, for you and for them. A smile softens even the angriest person.

When we start a new career path or venture out into unknown territory new people enter our lives. This requires you taking the leap to allow new experiences, and new people to come into your world. It requires that you talk to people. The most important thing I got out of that one encounter on that fateful night in my life was that there was a plan in motion far greater than I could see. There was a reason for every single person. There was a reason for every single situation where I came face to face with choice. Every person I've encountered in my life has had some sort of wondrous mystical presence and a hand in how my life evolved.

When you hear somebody say, "We're all connected" know it. When you look at another human being with anything else but kindness or compassion or delight, know that you're looking at yourself, because I know we're all connected. I know that without each single person, place or thing I've woven into my life I wouldn't be here writing this memoir. Sixteen years ago I walked down a path of wonder, trying to find answers to why this had happened to me. I got life changing answers I was seeking. The universe was quite blunt about it. It led to the questions, and for that, I'm so grateful. I've been following this path ever since. Every encounter truly matters.

"Always find time for the things that make you happy to feel alive"

-Author unknown

MONTH 4

WEEK 13: GRATITUDE ATTITUDE

"A moment of gratitude makes a difference in your attitude."

-Bruce Wilkerson

"Thank you, for thanking me, for thanking you, for the thank you note." My Father

My very first recollection of gratitude was at the age of eleven when my Mother had me write my first thank you note to thank someone for a gift. A week later, I got a note from the person thanking me for sending them a thank you note. I wanted to respond to them with another thank you note and then my Dad said, "No you can't. That would be like saying, *"Thank you for thanking me for thanking you for the thank you note."* This one saying stuck with me my whole life.

Gratitude at this level is actually required in our everyday lives. Showing appreciation for another or for a kindness that has changed a circumstance in your life sends the message to the universe that you know you have been touched angelically. Gifts come in all sizes and packaging and I'm grateful that I can now see how they aren't always in a box. I realized recently that everybody who walks into my world has a gift for me. That every experience I've had, even where I've had to look under the mud into the bottom of a scummy pond to find this gift, it was always there to help assist me in my future.

Letting someone know how they have changed your life or that of someone you love, changes two lives. It's the most important piece of the puzzle of life because when we say thank you from our hearts, it goes beyond the heart. It brings out the very depth of your soul and directly touches someone else's. When we are the giver and feel someone's sincere gratitude, it brings a joy beyond description.

For me gratitude goes beyond the thank you note. It's no longer about simply saying thank you for a gift. Gratitude is the life force that moves us through the gravest situations in our lives. I had no idea when I wrote that thank you note at the age of eleven just how impactful gratitude would be on the rest of my life.

Every time I want to challenge the universal decisions made on my behalf, I remember to have gratitude. I find some way to move me out of my own dooming thoughts with one thing to be thankful for, and I promise that every time I do this, my mood will change. I can look at things differently and remember that someone else has it worse than I do. When I'm feeling down about life's sometimes unfair circumstances, I go to gratitude, and it immediately picks me up.

What would happen if we were grateful for everything we have…every little thing you can think of? You have to start right there, because it's the little things and the big things and everything in between that keeps us alive!

My best friend told me she starts her gratitude train first thing in the morning by giving thanks for the hot water in the shower. Having gone without water a time or two I can relate to this luxury. Then she moves into having soap, shampoo, toilet paper, and clean towels. She then moves into gratitude for her morning coffee, and her ability to drive her daughter to school because she has a car. You see where this is going…

We don't always appreciate what we have today because we're always looking into tomorrow to see what we can get. Yet every single day of our lives, we have something to be thankful for.

Take a moment right now to look around and find something, however small, to be grateful for. Currently as I write, I'm grateful for the beautiful moon star solar light mobile that was my *"late in life"* high school graduation present from a dear friend. It hangs in my backyard with just enough color to send rainbow light against my fence in the dark of night, reminding me that I accomplished something I'd wanted to do for a long time. It's breathtaking.

When we find gratitude in the simple things, we open a door to everything. When we open the door to everything, we live as if it counts. The universe responds nicely to gratitude.

Finding gratitude isn't always easy when we allow the misery of just one day or one situation to cloud what we have in front of us. When I felt like I'd lost my career and felt I had nothing to live for, I had to dig deep to find gratitude. I found gratitude for the friends and family who were still there to boost me with their encouraging words. I was super grateful for my 401K savings account and the simple fact that I could hear music. I wouldn't have survived without music. I couldn't move much past that though, as I went through the days gloomily wondering how I'd live now, but those three things were enough to remind me to keep my head up.

When my daughter was diagnosed with an incurable disease we learned how gratitude could change our disposition about our situation by writing down three things every night in a gratitude journal. It helped us to find the light in a dark situation. We found gratitude for our doctors and our nurses, and the channels we were able to get on television in our hospital room. The letters she received from her classmates. My grandmother who funded my meals every day. When my purse was stolen out of her room and all my credit cards were gone, I found gratitude for sticking that $300 she gave me in my bra that afternoon instead of my purse. Concentrating on gratitude at the end of very long, unpredictable days is what got us through. For me it was also that my daughter was simply alive. For her it was simply that I was too.

In situations that seem to be the worst thing that ever happened to you, I can guarantee someone else has it worse. In those moments when you realize this one simple fact, you can exhale for a moment and know that gratitude will pull you out of anything.

When I was giving birth to my first child, after 36 hours of labor I grabbed the doctor by the jacket and asked him to move me to a hospital that would deliver this baby for me. I was then assigned for an emergency C-section. It was my first epidural and after the delivery I couldn't feel my legs for several hours. I wasn't prepared for the feeling of loss in my limbs. I laid there for five hours straight and all I could think about was how paralyzed people live every day.

Ironically, while in recovery, I was next to a man who had just been injured in a motorcycle accident. He was screaming, *"Ouch, ouch my leg, it hurts"* at the top of his lungs repeatedly for several minutes. I lay there silently thinking about how grateful he should be to be alive. When I could take no more, I looked over at him and said in my morphine state, *"Hey, I can't even feel my legs, you should be grateful that you can."*

Instantly, he stopped yelling.

We complain about our daily aches and pains when there are people who can't feel theirs. We complain about our jobs while there's someone standing in the unemployment line. We don't like what we see sometimes and complain, while there are people who can't see. We say we do not "like" this type of food and push our plate away when there are starving people all across the planet. I recently posted on Social Media to take the "go 24hrs without complaining" challenge and heard story after story of how that snapped them into gratitude.

We live in a 'more is better' society completely forgetting that there are people out there who have very little. One of my best friends and her daughters assemble care packages for the homeless where they live in Portland, Oregon. These bags are filled with homemade sandwiches, brushes or combs, toothbrush and toothpaste, handkerchiefs, power bars, fruit, and most importantly, love. They selflessly give their time and money to collect, buy, and drive around to the homeless people to let them know that they matter. I'm always so in awe of their selflessness and ability to give back. To me this is taking it to global gratitude status. Gratitude through sharing what you can give to someone less fortunate.

The University of British Colombia did a study that showed that people are happier when they splurge on someone else instead of themselves. Why? Because according to the study, "Being generous lights up the pleasure center of your brain and makes you feel more connected to others." What if each person on the planet did one kind thing, however small, for another person every day, and that ignited reciprocity for each of those persons, and so on? Then, what if everybody showed appreciation for those kind acts and the gratitude in each person began to grow and grow? What a happier world we would be living in.

In December 2012, after losing my job, I had no idea how Christmas was going to happen for my family that year. Then, Ann Curry started the #26actsofkindness born out of a terrible tragedy in Connecticut where twenty-six people lost their lives in the most random school shooting in history. It took off on twitter and went viral. I wanted in. This led to people all over the world spreading kindness to strangers' times twenty-six! It gave all of us a way to respond to this tragedy by spreading love instead of hate. My daughter and I brought twenty-six coloring books, twenty-six boxes of crayons, and twenty-six candy canes to the kids at UCSF. I was going through hell at the time, but we left with tears of joy in our eyes. We realized that this Christmas, although there may not be all the fancy bows under the tree, we had each other, and as we walked through the corridors of that hospital remembering our own experience, we couldn't help but feel gratitude for our own lives on a huge scale.

I believe that every single day we have something to be grateful for. It starts with the fact that I'm able to open my eyes. I'm grateful for the spirit inside of me that wants to get up every day and bring something beautiful and constructive to the world. I'm grateful for the ability to discern how I want to feel and how I want to show up to the world. I'm always grateful when I watch the sunrise.

Before I started this journey, I took many things for granted. My job: I never thought in a million years that I'd be fired, but in one hour, it all changed. My family: I thought they would always be there, then someone got cancer, and someone was hospitalized, and someone died. My friendships: Until I lost one. My home: Until fires broke out in Northern California and almost burned up the whole state. My health: Until my doctor told me my cholesterol was so high I'd fit neatly into a study for women in their fifties who die from heart attacks.

It all counts. Every breath, every choice, every sadness, every person, our security, our safety, and most importantly, our health. Every day I get another chance to be grateful. Take the gratitude challenge on the next page to get in tune with your appreciation for each person, circumstance place, or thing in your world. Write them out and let whoever needs to know you appreciate them, that you do.

Anthony Paul Mooji, a well-known spiritual teacher from Jamaica now based in London says it as simply and as effectively as I've ever heard: "Your mantra is thank you. Just keep saying thank you. Do not explain. Do not complain. Just say thank you. Say thank you to existence."

Questions to Ponder

- Who are you most grateful for in your life?

- Why?

- What would be a unique way to show them appreciation?

- What are you most grateful for in your life today?

  ○ Where in your life are you feeling unappreciated?

For the next 24 hours do not complain about anything. If you want to complain, come and write it here. Then tomorrow look at your complaints. See if it made any difference to your story by complaining about it.

For the next seven nights write down or invite your family to share with you at the dinner table three things you are grateful for. Then do it for the next seven days, and the next. After twenty-one days you'll be living in the grace of gratitude and your life will change. It will humble you and inspire you in ways beyond your imagination.

1.

2.

3.

WEEK 14: DON'T IGNORE THE SIGNS

"If you were waiting for a sign, this is it…"

-Author unknown

Have you ever looked through the rear view window of your life just long enough to see where you missed the signs?

Often in my life when I realized I ignored a sign, I think of the song by Ace of Base and sing it. *"I saw the signs, and it opened up my eyes… la te da,"* usually adding a little head bop to anyone who's watching.

The universe is constantly sending us signs. My favorite joke is called "God will save me." A storm comes into town, and the local officials send out emergency warnings that riverbeds will soon flood. They order everyone to evacuate. A faithful Christian man decides to stay citing *"I will trust God and if I'm in danger then God will send a divine miracle to save me"* The neighbors come by with room in their car. *"Nope, God will save me"* A man paddles by in a canoe. *"No thanks, God will save me"* Water pours into his living room and he retreats to the second floor of his house. A police motorboat comes by, and the man refuses, *"Help someone else, God will save me."* Finally, he has to climb to his rooftop to survive and a helicopter drops a ladder. *"No thank you, God will save me."* He's eventually swept away by flood and drowns. When he gets to heaven, he asks God, *"I put all my faith in you. Why didn't you save me?"* God said, *"Son, I sent you a warning. I sent you a car. I sent you a canoe. I sent you a motorboat. I sent you a helicopter. What other sign were you looking for?"*

The signs are always there. Sometimes it's that slightly off feeling you can't pinpoint, or a hard bang on the head ordering you to wake up. It's about recognizing the signs and listening to them. We make excuses for ourselves for each wrong move declaring, "Oh, if I only knew..."

When daily life is rolling by us at 55 miles an hour, we barely see the signs. We barrel through our busy days with a knowing, but often refuse to look. Yet, there's no question in my mind that every time I saw the sign, I knew it, I felt it, and I often waited far too long to act upon it.

How many times in your life have you known someone wasn't being honest, and no matter how much you pressed them they wouldn't budge, – but you knew?

How many times have you met somebody and the feeling was off but you pursued the relationship or the friendship anyway, usually with disastrous results?

A silent illness or sound awakens someone in the middle of the night just long enough to let him or her know something is very wrong.

Maybe you took the job knowing it wasn't what you really wanted.

I was twenty-one years old. I was in a relationship I knew wasn't working yet I somehow managed to get pregnant. In the late seventies it was still appropriate to plan the "shotgun" wedding after an announcement like this and while everybody was pretending to be jumping for joy, I was completely numb, looking at a future I wanted nothing to do with. I was marrying my drug supplier who I'd met at a bar. It was wonderful to party every night at the age of twenty, but the reality of that wasn't showing me the big picture. Still indoctrinated by society, I agreed to marry a man who I'd allow to control me and set me up for a season of insecurity and chaos. Two days before the wedding, I lost the baby.

I told no one but the Father and because we didn't want to let our families down, we went through with the wedding against every sign. I remember walking down the aisle of that little chapel in Tahoe unable to look at my Father and Mother yet still going through with the wedding. I knew with every cell in my body that I shouldn't have been marrying this man and yet I kept walking. That night I let it slip to my best friend that I'd lost the baby when I grabbed her champagne to chug in the bathroom stall. When my groom found out, he kicked a table in our hotel room so hard his toe broke. It knocked a glass off the table and I stepped on a piece of the glass and ended up needing twelve stitches in the bottom of my foot. Within four hours of the consummation of our marriage, we were in an emergency room treating dual foot injuries.

I had to call my parents, and then the doctor delivered them the news that I was in the middle of a miscarriage and I had to fess up to the truth. So within twelve hours of this monumental sign avoidance, the truth came out anyway, as my life coach Nancy Levin would say "sideways," and I was married to a man I didn't know if I could continue to love. I remember my Father's voice saying, "I knew something was off," and I remember my Mother saying, "You might have just made the biggest mistake of your young life." The feeling of knowing in that moment is like a memorable movie scene moment that has never left my mind or body.

However, as the universe provides in its almighty protective way, thirteen months later I was gifted with my first son whom I treasure more than life itself. Had I walked away that day, I wouldn't have him, nor my amazing three grandchildren. In that spirit, who's to say what would have happened had I walked away and it solidifies the saying "everything happens for a reason." Therefore, while I've never regretted that monumental ignorance because of these gifts, I've also never forgotten the feeling of self-betrayal and not listening to the signs. I believe that at this point of my life, the awareness of the signs has been my greatest gift. I've sung that song many times prior to making choices against my true self. Many further decisions in my life weren't lost on that experience because once you become aware of the signs and where they can lead, you're often able to listen next time.

I believe wholeheartedly in the Law of Attraction, and with that comes the bonus of awareness. When we're actively working towards manifesting our true dreams into our daily lives, a sign will always appear to lead us in the direction we're going. Serendipitous events become the signs that lead us to goodness.

When we're living consciously in our day-to-day lives, we're open to the signs and we make better choices. We stop searching and we start acting on the signs.

A phone call you answer instead of ignoring may change your world. An ever so slight pain in your stomach that prompts a call to your doctor for a routine office visit saves your life. A random newspaper advert that you hesitantly answer because you can't stop thinking about it, which leads you to your dream job. A missed highway exit that takes you to a different part of town where you meet the man of your dreams at a gas station. Something that makes you pull over and buy a lottery ticket, and you win. A song reminds you of that person you haven't spoken to in a long time and instead of just thinking of them something tells you to call and you call them and that's the last time you ever talk to them.

With six months to live, I wanted to make sure I was present for every sign because I didn't want to miss a thing. Each day I'm now more open to what's ahead of me. Sure, I plan "the day" but I'm always open to the changes and the alterations – the signs – that lead me to my next anything. Moreover, I listen to the signs. Life is a series of moments that are conspiring to bring you your best life. Our only part is to trust and listen to the signs and follow them instinctively with a sense of knowing.

Questions to Ponder:

What signs are you ignoring in:

- Relationships?

- Work?

- Friendships?

- Money?

- Where have you missed a sign and it led you to a moment you regret?

- Where have you listened to a sign with joyous life changing results that would not be a part of your life today had you ignored it?

- What can you do in each of these areas to manifest your true hearts desires?

List five things in each area that you want to manifest no matter how outrageous or out of reach.

(Here are a few of mine):

Relationships — *Close loving relationship with my children, my lover, best friends, and lots of fun and romance.*

Work — *Work primarily from home earning massive amounts of money and providing service to humanity in the process.*

Friendships — *Trusting friends who always support and cheer on my successes and have my back when I make mistakes.*

Money — *A flow of money to provide comfort, fun, home, security, and help anyone who needs it.*

Remember that after you do this, your only job is to look for the signs.

WEEK 15: OUR CHILDREN, OUR FUTURE

"Children will not remember their best day of television."

-Author unknown

There's nothing more daunting, challenging, and rewarding than being a parent. Parents feel a bond and a love for another human being like no other. Have you ever messed with a child and ignited a firestorm in their Mother? It's like no other furious bear in the forest. My daughter-in-law calls it 'breathing dragon fire.'

The surrogate, the step, the adopted, the auntie or uncle, and that one friend's parent who you proclaim, "I'm adopting you as my parent" walk with an unspeakable joy of bonding that one can see visibly in their interactions. Whether you're a parent by blood, or other circumstances, it's my deepest conviction that we as adults are responsible for the children.

Our children matter.

How we treat them, how we guide them, how we love them helps mold everything possible in their future.

Whenever I hear a parent gripe, "I don't know what's wrong with that kid," my inside voice whispers, "Look at yourself."

What was your role?

As busy working parents, we go through life doing for our children. We provide food, housing, transportation, we push for good grades, we barter for good behavior, we ground them (controlling) bribe them, threaten them, and forcibly try to change them to be the person we want them to be. When we've had enough we sit them in front of a television hoping we'll get five minutes of sanity back.

CHILDREN WON'T REMEMBER THEIR BEST DAY OF TELEVISION.

In that doing, being, forcing, threatening mindset, we fail to see who they truly are; whom they will be or want to become. Instead, we have the vision of who we want them to become. We press them early on to become a doctor, a lawyer, a nurse, or a firefighter. I remember trying to subliminally direct my daughter to be everything I wasn't. Yet in doing so, I failed to see who she really was, and who she wanted to become.

Many years ago when I was single parent raising a twelve year old and a five-year-old, I was so busy living that I failed to see any emotional upheaval in my children. I went through life thinking working and providing for them was enough. Hurry up, get home, do your homework, eat dinner, get in the bath, go to bed.

Therefore, I was surprised when the phone call came to tell me that my twelve-year-old son had been caught with a BB gun at school and was suspended. He was shooting it out the back of a truck.

This prompted "family therapy" sessions. Most often, the parents come in and are blasted for their role in how this child has turned out. "It's your fault," she said and asked me a question that would ultimately change the way I treated every child in the world.

How often does he play?

"Wait...what? There's very little time for play," I said.

"The only job your child has until he's responsible enough for himself is to play."

Twenty-five years later those words have never left my brain when interacting with children.

If you grew up in the sixties all you did was play. Cardboard sliding, doorbell ditch, hide and seek, role play, Peter Pan, chasing the pirates, Cowboys and Indians, cops and robbers, basketball, baseball, playgrounds...the list goes on. We rode our bikes everywhere, and we never returned home in the summer until the streetlights came on.

We went swimming at the community pool. We went to the beach to collect shells, the river to catch pollywogs, the lake to boat. We rolled down grassy hills on cardboard repeatedly.

It's common knowledge that now with video games, IPad, IPods, Iphones, tablets and headphones very little play is going on with today's children. They are plugged in and tuned out. Even a nine-month old baby is more interested in your cell phone then the toy in front of her. The average person's head is engaged in one of these devices 80 percent of the time – even as they eat – and also while they're watching television.

We have stopped playing with each other.

Your children won't remember their best day of television. Please go out and play with them. These are the memories we will all remember, talk about, and pass on generation after generation.

With six months to live I know that the only memory I want to leave my children and grandchildren is the joy of play. My grandson and I have a little game we play to find my mean old cat. The cat hisses at him every time, and it's the same game every time. He says: *Kiki, let's go see if Alvin's under the bed." For about a year I played this game. We would creep on our knees quietly, whispering while we peeked under the bed and promptly declare, "Nope." Yesterday, when I wasn't fully present with him he asked me to go look under the bed and I said, "You go." And then he said, "No Kiki, you have to come with me...it's our game, we're the cat detectives."* My world stopped, and I was on the floor with him in an instant.

I want to play with the children; to empower them, to explore their desires and deepest wants while they let imagination guide their reality. I want to play with my adult children to make up for every single time I was too busy to be there in the moment with them. I want to taste, feel, explore, remember, and breathe in every moment I have left with the people I brought forth into this world and their loving extensions.

Making memories is the greatest gift we can leave our children. Make today one of those "oh remember that day when..." kind of days. And, laugh and laugh and laugh.

My grandmother was still alive at the age of 105 years. She only had two children, but now she has twenty-nine grandchildren.

Yesterday I posted a video on my Facebook page where she was dancing around her living room still living life to the fullest. At the end, I noticed her going back to a place of play, singing ten times a day and dancing. A year ago she was almost dead in a hospital with pneumonia and flu, but her spirit – her playful inside person – wasn't ready to go. When I saw this video I was astonished and inspired to have known her and to witness the circle of life: Infancy to adult to infancy.

"Whether by action or spoken word, parents are the implements that write the story of a childs future"

-Randi G Fine

WEEK 16: HANGING ON VS LETTING GO

"Everything I ever let go of has claw marks on it."

-David Foster Wallace

Today I heard something very profound during the Deepak Chopra – Oprah Winfrey 21-day meditation on manifesting success, (day 18 to be exact). One of those sentences that knocks you in the face.

Oprah said, "We often think holding on makes you stronger, but the truth is, letting go is what makes you stronger."

I sat with that thought for a very long time. I know that I've "hung on" to people or things or circumstances many, many times in my life when I should have let them go.

We stay in relationships that don't serve us, constantly striving and struggling to "make them better." We stay at jobs we hate because we're afraid that if we quit we won't have enough money to make ends meet. We clutter our homes with things, hanging on to the pans from the yard sale down the street that we've never even used, or we just put things in a box and stack them in a storage unit never to look at them again.

When I picture the metaphor of hanging on, I see a person clenching their fists and hanging on a ledge for dear life using every ounce of strength they have to keep them there. When I picture letting go I see and feel the freedom of floating in air and flying effortlessly through my life.

There's usually great resistance to letting go of that person, thing or circumstance that's keeping you on the ledge. I found out the hard way that hanging on serves nobody.

I found out that if I surrender and let go of any outcome I'm clawing for, the universe will carry me through to my next person, thing, and circumstance effortlessly.

We cannot always control the outcome of our life circumstances. Hanging on usually means that's what we're trying to do. When we try to alter it with manipulation or with fortitude because we're "right" we serve no one. When we try to hang on to a situation that's slipping away from us, we're only fueling a smoldering fire.

Shamefully, I've been married twice. Both times when I left my marriage, it happened within an hour of making the decision. I packed up the things I could carry and walked out the door. In hindsight I should have planned both exits a little better, but what I did was subliminally learn how to let go. I just didn't know it at the time. The only thing I knew was that I'd lost all strength in the hanging on.

I hung onto a job that was physically killing my mind, body and spirit at the same time because I was a "team player," strong, and I could withstand anything the boss wanted to throw at me with a smile on my face. I cried every single day, I altered my life schedule to show people who didn't care about me that I was worthy. I neglected and jeopardized my health, my friendships, my family, and my relationships to hang onto a job that's only purpose in retrospect, was to pay the bills. Even though this was killing my spirit, I wasn't able let go.

Eventually, I was "terminated." I hung on for too long. It's likely that if I'd let go at the first sign of trauma and discomfort, I would have set a precedent for how I wanted to really live my life, which was free of all the discord that situation had brought me. By hanging on, I forced the universe's hand. I know that every person who's reading this can think back to a situation when if you didn't take the action to let it go, the universe stepped in and removed you, the person or the things you were hanging on to. No one is immune to this process.

When my house burned to the ground and I lost everything I owned, I had to let go. I had a large amount of cash in the house because in addition to not being able to afford fire insurance, I was afraid to put money in the bank.

I remember when my Father heard that the stack of cash had burned up in the dresser drawer, and watching him feverishly search the ashes for some resemblance of an unburned bill. I remember telling him to let it go. Everything was gone; I had ten dollars in my pocket. I bought a pair of dark sunglasses with that last ten dollars, perhaps to hide from the world after that terrible experience.

I was working for a man at the time who now goes down in history as the best boss I ever had. When I first got hired and he handed me our "employee handbook," which was a book called Conversations with God: Book 1, I knew I was in the right place. Back then I had no way of knowing how much he'd teach me about letting go. He was a master at it. As a gift after the fire, he gifted me with a one-hour therapy session with a psycho-therapist friend of his. I went in thinking I'd be able to rehash the story with her to "get it off my chest" and instead she taught me how to let it go. "Put an orange in your right hand and hold it out in front of you," she said. "Now squeeze it really tight." There I was, standing there clenching, "Think about the fire, the feelings you had, the turmoil that got you there...*AND NOW, DROP THE ORANGE.*" "There," she said. "Now doesn't that feel a lot better." One simple metaphor, and poof!

Every time I see somebody having a hard time letting go I tell him or her this story and I say, *"Drop the orange my friend, just drop the orange."*

I remember the moment of surrender, like a sweet glass of champagne. In retrospect, it was one of the most freeing moments of my life. Nobody likes to let go of money or his or her life possessions. Left with nothing, and you discover there's a peaceful freedom in allowing the universe to support you.

In each situation that I held on to for much longer than I should have, the only outcome was grief. I kept thinking things will change, feelings will change, life will change, people will change, when the reality is things don't change until you let them go. Life simply stays the same when you hang on.

Sometimes when I'm conscious of hanging on, I force myself to go to church. I don't think of myself as very religious, but when I look at Jesus hanging on a cross in a big wide open church, taking the blame for everything that may have happened centuries ago, I find comfort in surrendering. He was an innocent man, but he surrendered, let go, and let things evolve according to plan. He did not give one ounce of fight to having his hands nailed to a cross. He showed no defense, just acceptance of what was.

It also reminds me to take responsibility in the surrender of the letting go.

Part of the reason we hold on, is that we never want to admit we were wrong about a person or a job choice or that dress we had to have. I now see that letting go means admitting it isn't showing up the way I thought it would, or that it isn't serving me in any way. By letting go I'm opening up the possibility of something else more wonderful to come into my life than what I'm holding on to.

When we let go, we can live in the moment. We're not spending each moment worrying about the outcome of the next.

If you have six months to live, what's not serving you? What's worth spending your last days of potential life hanging on to? Every day is your last day. Everything you hang on to is robbing you of your inner peace on potentially your last day of life.

Learning to let things go will allow for a much happier existence. Don't hang on to things or people you can't control. Have faith in the process. Letting go = freedom. Freedom to make a new choice and freedom to unburden yourself from that unnecessary emotion called guilt. Or regret. Or self-sabotage.

Questions to Ponder

- What does "hanging in there" in any situation you have put too much into - accomplish for you?

- What am I hanging onto today that isn't serving me?

- What am I hanging on to today that's hurting me?

- What am I hanging onto that's cluttering up my life?

- Whom have I allowed to stay in my life longer than they should?

- When have I stayed in a situation longer than I should have?

- What would letting go feel like?

If you have something you are trying to let go of write down your most spontaneous thoughts, free of fear of the outcome, and describe what your life would look like if you just LET IT GO? What changes would letting go of this situation have in your everyday? Pick up an orange – think every thought, and then take the 'drop the orange' challenge!

I promise that once you bring it to the light, you'll be able to let it go and you'll never be the same.

> *"Sometimes letting go is an act of far greater*
> *power than defending or hanging on"*
>
> *-Eckhart Tolle*

No one wants to suffer. No one wants to be lonely. No one wants to live in fear. No one wants to lose everything. No one wants there heart ripped to shreds. No one wants to be sick. And no one wants to die. But these things happen in life. So the least we can do is be there for others, as we would like others to be there for us.

-Bryant McGill

MONTH 5

WEEK 17: THANK YOU FOR BEING A FRIEND

"Your truest friends are the people who don't walk out the door when life gets real hard. They actually pour some coffee and pull up a chair."

-Sandi Krakowski

I've been blessed throughout my life with the most amazing friendships on the planet.

I know that when I leave this world I'll miss them and they'll miss me. I know this because they let me know how much I mean to them. I know that we've exchanged gifts in this life that are unforgettable.

Our friendships start somewhere around the age of two. It's about then that you'll see a two or three-year-old grab the hand of a younger sibling or playmate and lead them into safety or teach them something new. I met my oldest friend at the age of one because our mothers were best friends. We stayed connected until they lost track of each other through life and both moved out of the infamous city, but forty-six years later when I saw her name on Facebook, I couldn't believe my eyes and I reached out. After much conversation we met on a beach in Southern California and it was as if no time had passed.

We walked back and forth on this little beach for hours discovering we had lived such similar lives, and the twists and turns and synchronistic timing of our "almost" encounters startled us both. At one time, we had lived blocks from each other and didn't even know it. She moved across the street from two of my best friends right after I'd left the area. Now, we talk all the time.

In that same spirit, I reconnected with some of my friends from middle school on Facebook and although we'd truly gone in different directions in our lives since the age of thirteen, something inside allowed us to plan a reunion in Phoenix. It was so outside of my box, as I hadn't flown for years for fear of crashing, yet something inside of me urged me to "just do it," and honestly that weekend added people into my life that I now couldn't imagine being without. We travel, we shop, we dine, and we explore, commiserate, giggle, drink much too much wine, and experience life we wouldn't have without each other. It may only happen three or four times a year, but the minute we're in the car together until the minute we arrive back at the airport we're in a friendship bubble that no one else can penetrate. It's easy and it flows. We're different and alike in so many ways.

The friendships I depended on in high school remain today. Even without Facebook, people would say to me, "You're the only person I know who has fifty friends from high school that get together regularly."

We were a group of beautifully complicated misfits trying to find our way in the most important years of our lives. We hung in a flock, usually thirty deep at the local shopping mall we called "The mag." It got its name because it was like a magnet that drew each of us to this central meeting place to experience friendship. This friendship bond continues today, with regular reunions where most of us are up to date with each other's lives. These people gave me the tools to survive. These are the friendships (you know who you are) that gave me a sense of family when I felt I had none. These are the friendships that I turned to in despair when I needed to run away from home, get off drugs, leave a marriage or a job, or change my life. I remember moving to Sacramento with two of my dearest sister friends, and for one whole summer we lived away from the life we knew to go and live with her parents. I was 17 years old, and we were caught shoplifting. This led to the police wanting to know where my "real parents" were. My parents knew where I was but in their eyes

I wasn't willing to live by their rules so I was a runaway. My friend's stepfather ran some crazy story past the security and somehow got me released to him. To this day I'm eternally grateful for his saving me that day. He made me call my parents and tell them, and that night when I went to sleep he put shaving cream in my shoes. The next night he short sheeted me, and the following night he put some awful smelling chicken in my suitcase. Just because he couldn't ground me he said, didn't mean I was going to go unpunished. I can't tell you how much we giggled then and now about that crazy summer in Sacramento. We bonded for life by a single summer.

When I was eighteen and had nowhere to live, my boyfriend's family took me in and I had become best friends with his sister. Long after he and I broke up, we remained loyal to each other. She showed and taught me the true meaning of friendship when she had to go against everything she knew inside to tell me her brother was cheating on me. It was the lowest and highest moment, because although I knew I'd just lost two people I cared about, I was gifted with the true meaning of loyalty and friendship. To this day, she's the person I most feel that not one second has gone by when we reunite. It's as if we just spent the last thirty years together. We have gone a year, sometimes two, without seeing or even talking to each other. She's my soul sister and we both know it.

When I moved away from my hometown to my now home two and a half hours away, I had no friends. It was the loneliest six months of my life. I decided to get a job at a local bar serving drinks and met the first person I'd call a friend in this foreign land in the Redwoods. That was twenty-eight years ago and I'm proud to say that she's still my friend. We had similar lives, family stories, and reasons to be out working at a bar every night until 2am.

Then I joined the local health club and starting teaching fitness. Through the friendships I formed there, I met my best friend. She was seventeen, and I was twenty-eight. We seemed the most unlikely pair, but to this day, we still call each other 'best friend.' We know unequivocally that we're there for each other under any circumstance. Through my best friend, I met five other fabulous women and we formed a dinner club called "The Bad Girls." Almost every month we get together for dinner, birthday love, and silliness beyond belief. I treasure these moments so much because their friendship is what has gotten me through everything in the last few years!

During my gotta make money somehow waitress days I bonded with two women who were actually much younger than I, only to discover the deepest soul connection between the three of us. We were 100% supposed to spend this time in our life together–growing, learning and supporting each other through the ups and downs of love – that we all seemed (ironically) to be going through simultaneously. There is certainly that one summer I know none of us will ever forget!

When I found myself in a position to need a lawyer after my life crumbled before me, I reached out to one of my little brothers long lost best friends and he became catalyst in my future and the writing of this book. I called, and in one minute – even from his vacation, he was making calls to negotiate my future for me. These types of friends? Irreplaceable.

How many times in your life have you reached out to a friend because you knew they'd be available to you for support? There's that one person you know that you can call at 3am for whatever you need.

Oprah has a great quote I recently retweeted on my twitter page @cathslife: "Lots of people want to ride in the limo, but what you want is someone who will take the bus with you when the limo breaks down."

This is what friendship is all about. It's about those people who make you feel at home wherever you are, and support you wherever you are in your life. These people don't judge you. They listen to you. They agree with you and validate you. They advise you when needed or asked. They play with you. They banter with you. They cry with you. They pick you up when you're down and afford you the same courtesy when they're down. They get you through heartbreak. I've come to realize that the reason our friendships matter so much is the ability they have to pull us through the darkest moments of our lives, and rejoice with us in some of the happiest.

I've learned that friendship has to be reciprocal. No matter how much time has passed we have to feel free enough to pick up the phone and connect with our friends. We have to allow ourselves to be vulnerable and truthful with our friends. There are times in our lives when friends are even more important than family because they aren't clouded by the family dynamic.

Years ago, I attended a creative writing class and was introduced to an exercise called "the inner circle." In this exercise, you make a circle in a circle in a circle in a circle. In the first circle, you put the names of people who have unconditional access to you. You answer their phone calls every time. They are the "yes I will drop everything" people in your life.

In the next circle, it's limited unconditional access. You will call them right back, knowing they'll understand when you see their call and you're busy, and you'll do everything possible to help when you can.

In the next circle, it's the limited access - period. The people you deal with every day, but you know definitely wouldn't ride in the bus with you. These people are usually co-workers, or friends of friends.

And so on.

Doing this exercise shows you exactly who's important to you and what direction you go in the event of a friendship needed heart attack.

It's a catch 22 (happy/sad) when you figure this out, but then you know who has your back in those 'I need you in an instant' moments, and who doesn't. You start to recognize how important that is in your life. Safety and comfort with another human being are lifelines to a happy life. We can get through anything with the help of a true friend.

With the theoretical six months to live "project" in full force it's so important for my friends to know how important they are to me. How they have shaped me. How they have helped me. I didn't want another minute to pass without them all knowing my gratitude for their roles in my life.

I was in a very precarious situation with the loss of my job because I lost so many friends in the process. I felt such grief stricken loss for them that it became part of the resentment I had for the situation. Here were people I'd stood beside every day, every Christmas party and summer BBQ, and I couldn't even walk back into my office and say goodbye.

Slowly, when the coast was clear for them to reach out to me, the truest friends called me. Some of them even gave me a "Jerry McGuire are you with me" moment by quitting after my demise, and some of them I sadly never talked to again.

I started my quest to acknowledge each friendship by sending a thank you card to my best friend. It was an old-fashioned thank you card that simply said 'thank you for being my friend.'

Then I reached out to an old friend because she was so heavy on my mind I couldn't stand it anymore and our conversation lasted for one and a half hours as we solved our problems together. I was so grateful for following my instincts. About an hour before the call she had been thinking about me. She said, "This is so weird." That call led to a dinner in which I and two of our other closest friends celebrated her sixtieth birthday. I was so honored to have this special milestone dinner with her. I wouldn't have had this moment had I not followed my urge to pick up the phone to call her that day.

We never thought we would celebrate a sixtieth birthday together, but here we were almost forty-four years later giggling and plotting like no time had passed. It was such a beautiful paradigm of life. Time usually changes everything, and time sometimes changes nothing. You know exactly what I'm talking about: the feeling that nothing has changed in spite of the circumstances or location of our lives having changed. We dined at an amazing Italian restaurant and laughed together. The feeling of knowing this beautiful person had been in my life since I was fourteen, and that forty-four years later I was still in her life had me crying tears of joy on my way home.

There were also two friends I knew I had to make amends with.

Then I planned several get togethers with my favorites. I wanted them to know time couldn't go on a second more without our connection.

During our commiseration about job loss, one of my friends and I created Blue Lakes Friday. Then when she started to work, again we switched it to her day off, Blue Lakes Monday. Any day that we could get together on a beach, relax, and share our life, even if it was for only two hours. We treasured these afternoons.

I called old friends and told them I missed them. I sent emails to people long missed. I visited their pages on Facebook to let them know I was thinking of them. I attended every wedding, party, bridal or baby shower I was invited to, instead of sending a gift. I started to nurture these friendships daily in some fashion, with a text emoji or a hug when we were together. My heart was getting fuller and fuller with each passing day. I felt like a silly little girl in high school because it was suddenly (to my entire family's dismay) about "my girls."

My friendships.

My life.

These are the people who will laugh and cry at my funeral. They will be the ones telling the stories that even my families don't know.

I can honestly say that friendship is one of the most vital aspects of my life in terms of fulfillment and survival. I often ask, where would I be without you?

For my whole life I've had the fantasy party in my head where I win the lottery and I'm standing on a stage handing out checks to "my girls" citing the gifts they've given me in my life and I'm humbled and honored to share my new found wealth with them. The song, "Thank you for being a friend "by Andrew Gold plays in the background. Stay tuned, as I have no doubt it will happen.

Questions to Ponder

- Write down the one person that you know is your ride in the bus with you – your do or die best friend.

- (If you are lucky, enough to have more than one add them)

- Ask yourself what you are doing to keep that friendship going?

- List your top five friendships and ask yourself what they bring to your life?

- Ask yourself how are you showing up and what are you contributing in each of your closest friendship's lives? And what they are contributing to your life?

- Where do you feel you cannot show up exactly how you are?

- What or who is holding you back from being authentic with these friendships?

- What situation or who do you feel you're judging and why?

- What situation or who do you feel judged by?

- Write down five people you haven't spoken to in the last six months that you can reach out to today with a simple, "thinking of you?

Let them know.

Do it today because you never know when it will be the last time you'll have a conversation with your friend!

#TL #BGC #LA #MARINADELREY #ENCINITAS #NYCITY #PORTLAND #PHOENIX #JUMP #WORTHY #WOW *I love you all more than any word on any piece of paper could say.*

WEEK 18: THEY SAY IT'S YOUR BIRTHDAY

"I want to be so distracted loving life, that I never realize I'm getting older."

-Angel Laney Sutton

I watched my twenty-six year old son dive into the water on his birthday to help a girl whose kayak had overturned at our lake dock where we were celebrating his birthday. She was clinging to the side of the dock by her fingernails trying to save her boat and there wasn't a person in sight who didn't feel her distress. My son used great strength to pull her up. I felt so much admiration for his spontaneous dive into the water, and for that split second I felt pride and gratitude for having given birth to him on this very day twenty-six years ago, if only to help this girl in her moment of need.

Every year on my first son's birthday, he calls me to wish me a Happy Birthday. For many years, I brushed it off as silly, but this year I took it to heart. Our "birth" days and their "birthdays" are the same. We get life, we give life, and this amazing circle of life goes around and around for centuries.

Often in my life I was cursing another birthday and the fact that I was "getting older" instead of being grateful for another day on this earth sharing life with people who bring me joy. John St. Augustine, broadcaster of the LIFE MATTERS podcast show on Play.it.com profoundly states, "we all know our birthdate, but our departure date is a mystery." He reminds us that we only have about 28,000 days on the average life span, so when your birthday comes around, it is a great reminder of what we have left. Knowing it is possible I may only have 7500 or so days left is a real eye opener to start living every day as fully as possible.

Being born around the Thanksgiving Holiday led to many overlooked birthdays in my house. My birthday would start with the Thanksgiving parade, so this became the only thing about my birthday that I enjoyed. It was further celebrated with a cake at the end of the big family dinner when very few people were excited about dessert, with the exception of my parents. Gifts were always forgotten in the holiday chaos. I went through most of my life being ok with this until I had my own kids.

That's when I started my own birthday traditions. My inner child came to the surface and I gave big.

I made sure that my kids felt honored on their special day. It would start with breakfast in bed until they were eighteen or left home. They loved this tradition, and have often shared it was the favorite part of their birthday, and they've since passed it on to their own children. My granddaughter always wanted a surprise party. In retrospect I suppose it was a cry for recognition, but we never gave it much thought, and we'd hide when she came home on her birthday night then jump out and yell "surprise!" We did that for years. At times she was so excited by this that we'd repeat it a few times in the night.

Birthdays are special because it's the day you chose to come into your life. It's a tragedy that we fear them or hide them to avoid having to admit our age. We sheepishly thank people for gifts as if we don't deserve them. Knowing how precious life is, I want to celebrate making it to see one more birthday. I want to hear horns ringing and see streamers streaming. My girlfriend Kim began a downward spiral as her fifty-ninth birthday approached. She was depressed and couldn't embrace that she was "getting older". She shares her experience with us:

Self-Talk Matters

I have never been one to be hung up on age. Age has been something I rarely thought about, perhaps because I have a young heart and spirit; until recently.

For whatever reason I decide my #1 bucket list was when I turned 60 I was going to celebrate my birthday on a beach south of France in a G-string topless; probably because I will never see any of those folks again. I always knew I had 2 years to get in shape which seemed.... doable.

Recently my brother was visiting and had just had a birthday and he was in town celebrating mine - going to a Rolling Stones concert (another bucket list). He made the comment "I can't believe I'm 57", I immediately said "Oh you are NOT 57" he interrupted and said "You are turning 59". I immediately called my older brother (11 months older than me with a birthday the following month). Franticly I asked him how old he was going to be. He replies "you're 59 sister I am going to be 60. In that moment my world crumbled. Apparently, denial was a suit I'd been wearing for a while.

The next few weeks I was in such a funk, not realizing why. On my birthday I was in a terrible space and it wasn't until I agreed to meet a friend at an AA meeting (long time member), and found myself watching the news where I saw a very terrible and tragic story. A young man in his late teens to very early 20's had just been sentenced to 18 years in prison for a DUI that killed 3 people.

As I was driving to the meeting feeling devastated for this young man, I realized how lucky I was to be driving to that meeting. Having been convicted of a DUI myself; I realized how GRATEFUL I was. That could be me. I could be dead or have killed someone else. What a gift my life is.

I left the meeting feeling a renewed sense of gratitude wanting to thank this young man for my epiphany. I realized my SELF-TALK became all about my age, time that I didn't have now to get in shape for France, another crushed dream. I allowed that one statement to rule my thoughts in a very negative way. I believe we are what we tell ourselves, we are responsible for our thoughts and our actions.

This may be a small illustration but the impact was big to me. After this epiphany, I spontaneously decided to do a 3 week walk on the Camino from

Portugal to Spain. I wanted to prove to myself that I could do anything I set my mind out to do, regardless of my age or my energy level. Here I learned to unplug, reset, spend some time getting to know my true self and just be quiet with my thoughts after what seemed like a lifetime of negative self-talk. What a gift of the unknown. The bonus plan of this self-seeking adventure was the toner body a journey like this affords. I now know deep inside that age? – Just a number.

Kimberly Nigro

Isn't this what our "birth" day is about? That one day in the year when we can celebrate whom we are, how far we've come, and reach towards our future by wishing on a candle. I always wished for somebody else. I only recently learned that it was okay for me to want things for myself. On my Grandmother's 105th birthday her wish was "for her family to be healthy."

I think about how many times I cursed my birthday and I have to laugh. Turning thirty was so depressing, until I turned fifty.

I now look at life so differently. A birthday means I'm still alive and I'm still able to make a difference in somebody's life. I'm still able to feel happiness and joy for another day. I now look at my birthday as an opportunity to see my year ahead and ask myself, "Where do you want to be next year at this time?" Then I have the opportunity to go for it. If I rob myself of one more year of wishing I weren't getting older, I rob myself of life.

Those days of our lives *need to be celebrated*. My life coach says, "Celebrate your successes," and your birthday is a successful day.

Using the premise of six months to live, from this point forward I will truly celebrate every birthday to the full. I went to the MACY'S THANKSGIVING parade a few years back to honor my birthday with some of my favorite people on the planet, and I think that's when this whole birthday thing started to shift for me. Six thousand dollars and ten days of fun in New York was more than amazing. As I sat on the corner of Seventh Avenue waiting for it to start, along with thousands of others, a man from Jersey announced to the immediate crowd that it was my birthday. Before I knew it, five hundred people from every corner sang Happy Birthday to me. Even the police officers joined in. Talk about a memorable birthday moment!

I deserved it! And so do you. Birthdays matter!

Don't look at the wrinkles, the gray hair, the changing body, and the circumstances of your life. Make way for your big day in a big way. Nothing would make me happier than to start a birthday revolution where people across the country start celebrating their life large. One of my dear friends celebrates a birthday month. We can start with ourselves.

I took on this cause for myself and planned the perfect birthday party for myself, which looks something like this:

It's Thanksgiving Eve on Blue Lakes beach. The weather is unseasonably warm. It's 3:30 in the afternoon when my guests start to arrive. There are torches in the sand and the guests are dressed semi-casual to dressy. Shoes are optional. There's a long table in the sand with enough chairs for forty of my favorite people with beautiful blue bows tied on the back. Heaters surround us. There's the sound of gentle waves in the background and the wildlife is quiet. The plates are made of china and the glasses are crystal. The silverware is oversized. The table décor is modern and funky with a blue and white color scheme with a splash of light pink roses in vases down the middle.

Fresh lavender is strategically placed for aroma. The water glasses that are filled with ice, lemon wedges, cucumber and mint, are the deep blue hard clear glass kind. Appetizers include large shrimp cocktails and a complete bruschetta bar; an amazing cheese filled platter with grapes, crackers, and yummy surprise me hor'dourves. For dinner, we're having Filet Mignon and Lobster and BBQ Turkey. There is crunchy sourdough bread slightly warmed with grass fed butter. Also, fresh spinach and grilled asparagus, truffle fries, and a huge green salad of mixed greens, kale, strawberries, blueberries, peaches, avocado, goat cheese, and lemon dressing. For dessert there's chocolate cake with white buttercream frosting (the good wedding cake kind), and vanilla bean or peppermint stick ice cream. Plus, there's pumpkin cheesecake for the non-chocolate lovers (if they exist). We'll serve champagne and sparkling cider, sparkling water, fine red Mendocino County Zinfandel, and good brew beer. Hot coffee espresso bar for everyone is after dinner wishes. We mingle, we talk about each other, we love, and we laugh until we cry. We watch a magnificent sunset and light the torches. The DJ comes onto the beach and we have a dance off. Of course, my best friend wins and the grand prize is a day at Disneyland with me!

From my family I'm gifted (finally) with a diamond tennis bracelet. I've been in a family of jewelers for my entire life and have been waiting for that darn bracelet! The party continues the next day down the I-5 to celebrate in my happy places in SOCAL. Thanksgiving is spent on Zuma beach in Malibu with dinner at Kristi's restaurant. On Friday, we hit Huntington for a full day at the beach. I rest on Saturday and hit Disneyland on Sunday and Monday. Finally, I get home on Tuesday.

Honestly, just writing this was exciting. If you felt any part of that then you know how special a birthday can be. WRITE YOURS OUT JUST FOR FUN!

MY PERFECT BIRTHDAY PARTY:

WEEK 19: MI FAMIGLIA

"Family is not an important thing, it's everything."
-Michael J. Fox

When you walk into my brother's home, the first thing you see is huge wooden letters across the family room wall, spelling out, "FAMIGLIA." Every time I see it, I'm reminded that I'm Italian, but more importantly that I have a family that loves me and means the world to me. A family that accepts me exactly as I am. Of course if I'm messing up, they have no problem telling me, but they've also always had my back.

We celebrate our Christmas Eve's at their home. It's one of our most treasured family times of the year. These evenings have included such things as a horse carriage ride through the streets of their tiny town to see all the decorated houses with lights and Christmas cheer. It's pure magic, and a tradition that my children will always remember. Stop for a moment and think back to one of your most treasured family memories. There's such an indescribable feeling of home that it's hard to describe.

Holiday gatherings are an important part of growing up in a family. It is my true belief that family traditions we create at holiday time can be the most memorable times of your life. There was always a stray person at our Thanksgiving or Christmas table who didn't have a family to join on those days. I was always fascinated by them. My grandmother would carry in 5 big white boxes wrapped in a big red bow- filled with different goodies every Christmas Eve when we were children.

We would reminisce about the times before, laugh and eat too much, and gather around televisions to watch football. It's the time of year to get in touch with the warmest feelings we have for our family members.

Treasure these moments like your last breath! These are the best times of your life!

Through this journey, I realized that although those three or four days a year were sheer magic for me, with the theoretical six months to live, they wouldn't be enough. I would want to spend even more time with these people! Like an attached limb, without them I lose my purpose.

When a family member unexpectedly leaves us, a hole is individually ripped through each person. It leaves us all shattered in a different way and there's nothing to do but grieve alone. As we did when our Mother died. The family home was sold, our Father moved on, and those memories became ever so important to keep some semblance. I'm so grateful for the ability to continue coming together, sharing our families and our lives, and keeping traditions alive for our children.

Family breeds familiarity. I feel drawn to these people like no other. It isn't even so much the blood bond as the feelings behind the bond itself. We learn and grow from infancy with these people and everything in their lives that happens, affects every one of them and you. Like a team.

Add a family trauma to this mix and you witness the pulling together of family. During a recent trauma in our family, I said to my brother, "Wow, we really have coming together down." And he paused and said, "Sadly, it's usually some tragic event that pulls us together." That's so true.

We love to share the highs, but nothing brings family together like the lows. I like to think of my family as my "tribe." My Granddaughter is Indian and life with her is always one big dance around the fire. Her free spirit reminds me that she's on her own clock, doing her own thing, and that although we're related, we're different souls on an individual journey. Yet she chose us, and we're family.

In my immediate family we talk a separate language so no one can understand us (rab-all-abeey webeedab-ooo). At one time we gauged how people from outside the tribe would fit in if they caught on to this garbled language quickly or not. If they could speak and understand it, they were worth keeping around, as if they belonged.

Family is an absolute need in our lives. The one constant. Family bring out our greatest, most joyous feelings.

Like witnessing the first-born girl in a generational family of boys.

Who doesn't love a big wedding? When I witness the families at a wedding, from the father - daughter walk down the aisle, holding back tears, to the best man toasts, the first dance for a new husband and wife, and the last dance for a father and his daughter, I'm always overwhelmed with the love in the room. Then the dancing begins. There are no inhibitions, no one cares what Uncle Al or Aunt Betty look like, everybody just goes for it. Celebrating the beginning of a new family and a joining of families is remembered forever.

Holidays, birthdays, vacations, and summertime fun are all so special. Family traditions handed down from generation to generation to keep the spirit of those passed to continue on and on and on. I don't know a mother on the planet who doesn't have a special ritual that's only done with her children. Children love traditions.

Our family's structure helps to create us. We identify with each other.

We plan together, and when something wonderful happens who's the first person / people you want to tell? *Family.*

Likewise, when something goes terribly wrong, we usually call family.

Our family is there for us even when all they can do is hold our hand. They will bail you out of jail, pick you up from the hospital, defend you even if you're wrong, and love you when you're against the rest of the world.

Family can also bring us to our knees, absorb our energy until we have no more, make us feel unimportant, challenge us, betray us, ride us, point out our faults, frustrate us, and challenge our very existence. Family makes you act out embarrassing raw behaviors formed through our interactions when we were too small to remember.

When I was fourteen, my brother, who was twelve at the time, knocked the wind out of me with one solid punch to the stomach. The scene has played in my mind a thousand times. When I was sixteen, I picked up a huge milk crate and heaved it at my seventeen-year-old brother's brand new car in anger. Denting the hood and nicking the windshield, I have no idea what my brother did to incite such behavior in me — or where my parents were to allow this, but the memory carried no memorable consequence. I was forgiven, because I was family. Now we laugh about those moments, sometimes hysterically.

Being born into a family of boys created the tomboy in me but to this day hitting and throwing doesn't fit who I am. For the longest time I thought I was adopted. I created the scenario that my Mother couldn't have girls so they secretly snuck me into the mix.

Two years ago when connecting with a long lost friend who everyone referred to as 'my twin sister' growing up, I thought, *"What if it comes out that we're actually sisters, and that our parents had an affair?"* I laughed, and thought, *"Where in the world did that come from?"* Was it so bad to be in my own family?

It was a trying time. We had been only scratching the surface around the pain of losing our Mother even though fifteen years had passed. Our Grandmother was heading into her early one hundreds and our Father had moved away in the aftermath of our Mother's death, choosing to live life on his terms. It seemed we were so disconnected, yet the holidays, graduations, and birthdays brought us together about four times that year and then our Grandmother got very sick. This woman had been in our life for sixty of her one hundred and five years; the one constant we could count on.

But at the age of one hundred and five, with pneumonia and the flu, it looked like her last days were ahead of us.

Unanimously, we came together and within three weeks we had her house stripped and cleaned, her finances in order, 24-hour caretakers and everything she'd need to transition her home. We never spoke about what needed to be done; we just did it.

It's important to grasp and appreciate these moments while you're alive. While they're alive. These precious moments of connection with our loved ones are gold and they're what you will remember when you're at the end.

Although my education on the subject of death tells me that when our loved ones die they're with us whenever we need them, I still never want to lose a single one. Faced with the awareness that I will, I want to appreciate and treasure each one of them like I will lose them tomorrow. I want them to know that I'll always be there. I want them to feel my joy and hug me through my pain. And I want to be there for them in the same regard.

Today, pick up the phone and call one of your family members. Today, tell them you love them and make a plan. If you don't have a family tradition start one as soon as possible. It's never too late.

Here's what I know for sure and what prompted me to change everything about the way I took my family for granted: In an instant I knew one of them could be taken out of this physical existence and I'd never be able to say, "I'm sorry, I love you, I forgive you, forgive me, or I appreciate you." And if any of those emotions are still lingering when they decide to go, I'll feel incomplete.

I tell them now regularly, every time I talk to them. I leave them with "I love you." Every time they need me I let them know I'm here.

From the endless laughter when we're together, to the bond of love like no other, I have a family.

Questions to Ponder

- What is left unsaid to one of your family members that you would want them to hear before you die?

SAY IT HERE

- Who in your family do want to know that they're so very special to you?

TELL THEM TODAY.

- Who in your family are you in discord with and what action step can you take to heal it?

You need to do this before it's too late.

- What tradition do you have in place that warms your heart and brings you closer to your family?

- What tradition would you like to start?

START IT TODAY.

Do not let time slip by you without letting your "tribe" know you love them or that you forgive them.

As cliché as this may sound in a book like this, life is too short to hold onto grudges or take personal stands against a member of your tribe. As Elizabeth Gilbert wrote in Eat, Pray, Love about letting go of the anger and resentments that linger in a bad relationship, "Send them light and love and let it go."

With any time left to live, do you really have a choice?

WEEK 20: CHOICES = CONSEQUENCES

"You have a choice. A single choice, whatever that choice may be, you have to live with the consequence it brings. That is all. A choice."

-G. Gutierrez

Just the word consequence makes me cringe. I look around my everyday life and I know that consequences exist, lurking around every corner, in every aspect of my life. In its simplest definition, we make choices, and those choices lead to consequences.

Often, when a lesson is involved, the lesson in the consequence will outweigh the ease of the choice. To make a choice is relatively simple. Even if we hem and haw about a choice, eventually we just make it. More often than not, I've found that my choices can be very spontaneous. What I lacked my entire life wasn't the ability to make the choice, but I lacked the ability to see the consequence up front.

I normally operate in a "spur of the moment" mind frame; a 'throw caution to the wind' kind of mentality. I had to look at the negative consequences that many of my life choices brought in, in order to find peace in this process; in order to let them go and begin to live fully without regret.

I always envision a big hammer coming out of the sky and a loud voice saying, "Now you've done it. Here's your consequence, Cathy, *your karma.*" Alternatively, that of a parents' voice saying, "I told you so." I shrink to the size of a mouse squeaking, "Why in the world did I do this?" It's a feeling; a stomach-turning feeling inside.

A provocative internal question of, why did I make this choice? Sometimes consequences are unspoken, and sometimes they're louder than life. On this journey to live as if each day mattered, I knew I had to find a way to learn how to think first and teach myself the ability to foresee consequences for my choices in the future. I also had to remember that I'm only human.

Here's a few from my list:

CHOICES with consequences…

I moved twenty-three times from the age of seventeen to twenty-eight.

I fought with my mother every day of my teenage years. When she died, I'd only had ten years of relationship with her that I remembered as loving.

I left a job way too soon that would have given me a retirement package for the rest of my life because I let my pride and wounded ego do the talking for me.

I spoke up for myself and the battered women before me and I lost my lifetime career job, which led to losing friends I had for years. I made a choice on one day, in one second, with one sentence, and my world turned upside down. In the end though, I held my head high in spite of the consequences. When you stand up for yourself, you achieve an unexplainable power inside. You need no validation for who you are.

I loved too much. I overpowered another person's life with what I thought was right for them (namely me) and it led to resentment rather than reciprocal love. I didn't allow them to be who they really are, pushing, pulling, and attempting to make them who I wanted them to be – and I pushed them right out the door.

I loved too little. I hurt another human being because I couldn't get out of my own way enough to see the love this person had for me. Love isn't always on the same level between individuals, but to bypass someone's love for you or take it for granted taught me to believe I wasn't worthy of being loved that much.

Any choice we make will always have a consequence. Therefore, in the spirit of having six months to live, I also thought it important to give merit to the consequences in a positive way, to see the wills of my ways and understand that life is about choices – and all choices have led me to this moment. By doing this, I'm able to see the gift of each choice I made in my life. I can find its place in the evolvement of me, and continue my quest for living with inner peace.

If I hadn't moved twenty-three times, I wouldn't have the gypsy soul I carry around with me everywhere I go. It has served me well in many instances on my journey. I wouldn't have the ability to pick up and go anywhere, meet anyone, and make friends everywhere.

I also wouldn't have learned how important having a sense of family and home really is to our spirit. I wouldn't have learned how vital it is to be comforted in one place and feel serenity in that one place you can call home. By moving around as I did, I found that the most important thing to me is having a home where everybody feels comfortable; a place you don't have to leave unless you want to; a place you know will always be there and that you're always welcome there.

Having a place my children can identify as home has always been super important to me. I didn't feel that as a child. Recently, I went on a solo vacation for ten days, which I've rarely done throughout my whole life. When I got home, my adult daughter and my granddaughter came to stay with me for three days. They sprawled out on the couch, turned on Netflix, ate food, and looked at me and said "AHHHHHH, Mom's home. I haven't felt this feeling for days." That was what I'd searched for my whole life and I'd been able to give them the gift of a feeling of home. It's truly what we all need and deserve.

If I hadn't fought with my Mother the way I did, I can honestly say I wouldn't be the Mother I am today. It was important to me that along with being a parent guiding and teaching them through their lives, that they also felt loved and wanted. I made the quality of our interaction and our daily relationship more important than the homework or trouble at school. Losing my Mother so quickly

143

expedited the process of loving them unconditionally because I didn't want to leave this planet feeling the regret I felt. I miss my Mother beyond words and in my chapter on regret I tell you how much I regret the fighting and rebellion, but I also know that she taught me some valuable lessons on love in the middle of all the strife. In the end, that's what mattered the most.

Leaving the phone company was a big mistake. I'd worked there for five years and was put on probation for laughing in the background with my best friend while a customer was on the phone. This led to the union fighting for me to keep my job. I was awarded seven months of back pay and full reinstatement of my seniority. I was twenty-three years old. If I'd stayed there for five more years, I'd still be getting a check from them today, and my stock, that I sold for so little back then, would have taken care of me for the rest of my life. Instead, I went back into my office with a crowd cheering and we all wore our sunglasses rebelliously in unification of the union's victory. I waited three weeks and walked out with my middle finger in the air as if I'd just won something. WHAAAAAAAAAT? I couldn't see the consequence of this choice at the time. No one told me, "If you stick this out you'll have money coming in forever." So, what was the good? If I hadn't have done that I wouldn't have met the father of my children. I went on to move to the countryside, and have two children who lit up my life in ways that a paycheck cannot. That, however, is the only good thing, because if you're still reading this I want you to know one thing: RETIREMENT IS VERY IMPORTANT! SAVE YOUR MONEY, INVEST YOUR MONEY, and prepare for your financial future even if it is just to leave it for someone else. That was my lesson.

If I hadn't spoken up, I wouldn't have learned the power of my strength. If I hadn't spoken up and said "enough of this" I wouldn't have found myself in the position to catapult my life forward, even though I had no idea where I would go.

If I hadn't spoken up, I'd still be living in a turned off emotional plane operating on autopilot to function. I'm quite sure I'd also be stressed out to the max, overweight, and gray.

If I hadn't spoken up, I wouldn't know peace.

If I hadn't loved too much, I'd never know what it feels like to love with my whole heart. I wouldn't know that my heart could withstand anything. And I also learned about surrender.

I used to have a saying that went like this: *"Break my arm if you will, but please don't break my heart."* Anyone who has had his or her heart broken knows that it's the most painful feeling in the world. When we love a child, a spouse, a parent, a sister, a friend, we know the power of love. It may have hurt me to love that much and then lose, but I'm so grateful to know the feeling of love.

If I hadn't loved too little, I can honestly say I wouldn't know what it's like to be loved. I wouldn't know what it feels like when someone looks at you so adoringly. Nor would I know the feeling of being wanted and desired. By stepping away from love, I learned so much about it. When a person gives you their love and their heart and you misuse it or discard it and hurt someone, it hurts you. The guilt and the shame around how I might have shown up in a relationship with less enthusiasm and knowing that it hurt someone changed the way I interact with everybody. I learned through this process that we all deserve as much love as we can possibly call into our lives. I know after hurting someone that I can never do it again. I've learned that I can't lead people into believing something that isn't true, or hold somebody back out of selfishness.

I'm grateful for every choice: good, bad, or ugly for the simple reason that this means I've lived. Life is about choices, and now that I come face to face with the realization of how each choice I've made has affected my life, I'm very cautious. I'm more thoughtful now about what the consequence will be if I make a choice. Life is about learning as you go, and by identifying your choices and their impact, you'll live a happier existence because you'll have less regret.

Questions to Ponder

- What are the top life changing choices I've made and what has been the negative impact on my life?

- What has been the positive impact? Find the good, because I know it is in there.

- If I only had six months to live, what choice could I make today to feel the best for my future?

- What one thing have you been wobbling on the fence about that you can make a choice about today one way or another?

- Write down the negative and positive impact it will have on your life?

If you do not want to write it down, say it aloud. Sometimes when we bring awareness into our reality we can't look back. By saying it aloud, or writing it down, you have told your inner self how these choices have influenced you and what the consequences are. You end up polishing your choice button for the next choice to become clearer. What I know is that choices arise every day, which affect our health, our financial wealth, our worthiness, our tribe, and our lives. I want to remain conscious in my choices from now on. I want to be present, and I want to be happy about the choices I make.

"Isn't it crazy how we can look back a year ago and realize how much everything has changed? The amount of people who have left your life, entered and stayed. The memories you won't forget and the moments you wish you did. Everything. It's crazy how all of that happened in one year " Author unknown

Found on the Facebook page - Sarcastic Bad Bitches via Facebook

"I wish I'd said all the things I never got around to saying to my friends and extended family. I wish I'd confessed the secrets I was holding. I wish I'd told some people how much I loved and appreciated them. I wish I'd told my daughter how sad I felt that I had broken promises to her"

-Gay Hendricks – 5 wishes

148

MONTH 6

WEEK 21: THE PATH TO SELF-LOVE

"I don't have to look for love because I am love."

-Euphoria Godsent

If you've ever been in love, you know that for the first three months or so you're giddy, light, and downright euphoric at times. You feel butterflies in your stomach and you can't think about anything else but this lustful, vibe that feels bulletproof. Who can dispute that it feels good to be in love? Love increases levels of oxytocin in the body, which increases dopamine, and makes you feel happier than any drug can. You look forward to everything about this person, doing as much as you can to please them.

Then, real life sets in. Behaviors show up in one another, which you couldn't see in the blind state of love-ness you were feeling. Bills have to be paid; children need to be tended to. Career choices get in the way, with one or more persons wanting more "time" with the other. Past relationship pain can find a way to resurface, and often this "in love" feeling begins to crumble before your eyes.

If you then break-up with this person who you couldn't live without three months ago, you go out and spend more of your precious lifetime trying to rediscover that in love feeling.

Again.

And, again.

We have all been there as we seek a love outside of ourselves. The bonus plan is that someone else is responsible to keep it going for me.

I have to be honest. Self-love was something I'd always heard of, and had no idea how to grasp.

"If you want to truly love someone first you have to love yourself." Or a constant quote reminder: "Self-love is the best way to find true love."

The Buddha profoundly quotes, *"You can search throughout the entire universe for someone who is more deserving of your love and affection than you are yourself, and that person is not to be found anywhere. You yourself, as much as anybody in the entire universe, deserves your love and affection."*

I heard the words and had no clue what they meant or how to implement a plan like this. I was sure I rather liked myself. I thought I looked good on occasion, when I dressed up. I went out of my way to help others and I felt generally happy. Then my critical voice would start to talk to me and was always so much stronger.

"You just look sleepy. Older. Tired. Whoa girl, your wrinkles are really showing today. If only your teeth were whiter. You'll never have a bikini body. You're stupid for thinking you can pull this off. You never graduated from high school, so who's going to take you seriously? You lost your career because you couldn't keep your mouth shut. You lost your shot. You're older now, you can't wear that! Nobody is going to want you."

It took me months of excavating all the negative self-talk and consciously counting out all the times I had these silent conversations with myself. I began to grasp that some of the thoughts I had about myself, I'd never say to somebody else.

So why would we ever talk to ourselves this way? It could be that as you grew up you were told you were worthless and you built a negative belief about your self-worth. Or it could be your today reality because you've surrounded yourself with narcissistic people who don't value you. I came to understand that my self-criticism and self-loathing was damaging my ability to love myself.

It took a huge shift and a lot of hard inner work to find self-love.

I challenged myself to "just notice" every time I talked negatively about myself, and then I took it further and tried to "just notice" when I talked negatively about somebody else. I took that one step further and started to "just notice" when I talked negatively about anything. Osmosis kicked in when I began to notice when other people were speaking negatively as well. This one exercise was life changing. When you begin to notice your behaviors, you can change them.

My path to self-love started with a group of girls I didn't know. I signed up for an online coaching group called *"Jump and your life will appear©"* facilitated by author, mentor, life-coach, and friend, Nancy Levin. Although I'm not generally a quiet person, in the beginning I was a shy, inhibited, insecure woman with absolutely no idea how I'd got the courage to join this group, let alone speak my truth to them. Vulnerability wasn't my strong suit. Riddled with confusion about the life changes I didn't ask for; how could I tell anybody a truth I didn't even know myself? Three groups later I can honestly say I'm at the finish line with my arms up in victory, though I'm definitely not done jumping into my life.

We unraveled through a process of looking at ourselves authentically, excavating the layers of beliefs that held us back. We gradually gained the courage to "jump" into our new lives with confidence. I had to uncover and understand why I had allowed myself to stay in so many situations throughout my life where I was demeaned or made to feel inadequate for a paycheck or a false sense of security. I wanted to uncover the fears and answer for myself why I had lacked the courage, and what I now know to be self-love and self -worth, to walk away from anything that didn't serve me.

With six months to live, the only thoughts of the utmost importance, was that I was happy!

In situations where emotional abuse is tolerated, we can develop a numbness inside that, although can be visibly seen from the outside, often nobody will say a word. They silently witness your behavior changing and grapple with their own misplaced feelings about it. You develop an immunity to the damage it is causing.

I had no idea how much damage had occurred inside of me until I was away from it. I remember the honest concern on the faces around me, as my life crumbled from a voice of authority that was keen on proving to everyone that I wasn't "worthy" of the position I was in. I'd devoted night and day in this one situation and then one day vanished. That degrading experience led me to seek answers on how I could avoid that ever being my reality again.

Slowly, with the help of women I only knew through a Facebook picture and a voice on the phone, I felt an opening in my soul and began to share my sincere self with strangers. These women would go on to be eternal soul sisters.

To identify my tolerance for abusive behaviors that didn't serve me, I started to retrace all of my past powerful relationships, primarily with the men in my life, from family to boyfriends to bosses. Coming from a family of boys that wasn't an easy process. Our first relationship is with our parents, then siblings and family, and then the outside world. I fought physically with a couple of my brothers throughout my life because they fought with each other. It was acceptable at the time because we were children, but in retrospect I never stopped and separated it for what it was, which allowed it to be okay in my adult life.

Each relationship that triggered undervalued feelings in me, suffocated my ability to see myself as worthy of being treated with respect, treated as an equal, or treated with the reciprocal kindness and love I was giving. I was a people pleaser first, co-dependent as hell, and willing to go beyond for many of the people in those relationships that now I could clearly see didn't value me at all. I unraveled me. I shared personal feelings and emotions in their rawest form while others did the same, and we transformed.

I attribute much of my self-love transformation today to Nancy Levin and these beautiful women for guiding and inspiring me through each step of my path.

I tried on "authentic happy Cathy" with them. By exposing my fears, listening to theirs, and witnessing their own paths to self-love I was transformed. I wanted to know what my life would look like if every day I was happy, no matter what. What if I chose to be happy instead of allowing my life-long conditioning to look for the fearful or negative outcomes? What if I simply surrendered in situations I didn't have any control over?

I started walking around with ear buds in my ears every morning listening to Abraham Hicks on You tube. It opened my heart to the law of attraction and drove home a single point that shot straight to my soul...that self-love held the key to everything being in perfect synchronicity in your life.

Self-love doesn't mean you love anybody else less. It means you're taking control of your own life and making things happen for yourself without depending on another person. You pick yourself and your feelings first so that you're in alignment with your truth. The universe takes care of the rest.

The best definition I've ever read about the relationship meshing of two people in *and* staying in a complete state of self-love was in the book written by Neale Donald Walsh, Conversations with God Book 1 – Relationships, chapter 8. I think I read it ten times because I loved the way it described two people perfectly blending emotionally and physically. He used two subjects called Tom and Mary and they became "ToMary." Today we see this couple name meshing everywhere, and I always attributed that chapter to the craze. But even in this chapter, "God" acknowledges that two people have to come together as two individual self-loving people. One cannot be dependent of the other, worry about what the other is doing, saying, being, or becoming, only to be themselves.

If you want to see the definition of what I believe a true love relationship is, read that book, and chapter eight specifically.

I then consciously looked only at the positive. One of the exercises in our group was to "say no for 24 hours to everything." This was life changing because you have no idea how many times you say yes until you can't say yes.

I took it a step further and asked myself when faced with decisions that required me to choose, how does this serve *my* highest good?

Our life coach Nancy Levin shared a self-love morning practice of asking herself first thing in the morning, "What's the most loving thing I can do for myself today?" The first time I tried this, I got the answer "exfoliate." I laughed, but then realized I barely took time to wash my face through my rushed life.

We often put other people or things before ourselves and this one practice leads us away from self-love. I can assure you my tribe wasn't happy with "new self-loving Cathy." Here was an unrecognizable woman who was always saying yes against every cell in her body, now saying no, no matter what. It was the hardest on people who were used to me always putting them first. Particularly, the people I shared life space with.

I began to live on my own time clock, with my own opinions, my own wants, and my own needs being met by only me. It didn't mean I was ignoring them or their needs, it just meant that mine were now equally as important as theirs. When you spend your life teaching people that you put them first, it takes a bit of undoing. However, stay true to yourself, as this is an important part of the process. For me there's no other way to live your life other than to put yourself first.

To all the Mama's: I get that cannot always happen. I raised three children and have four grandchildren I'd drop everything for. It just means to remember to fit yourself in, too!

By saying no for even twenty-four hours I learned to feel what was right for me. By putting myself first in each situation that I had to ask myself yes or no to, I could relate to my truest feelings about each situation. This is what led me to learn how to love myself, simply by putting my feelings first. It showed me what was most important in my daily life.

In the next three weeks of my life I did nothing but what was right for me even if other people showed resistance. Imagine the conflict my tribe felt. The reward was a feeling I'll never forget. Everything felt so right that I could never go back to people pleasing again. It was a huge shift, because then it became about giving kindness to another and not something I had to do to make them stop or start acting a certain way.

When I do something for somebody else from my heart I feel warm from head to toe. When I'm not acting from this place, I feel anxiety from head to toe.

Self-love now feels simple. Love yourself and treat yourself in the same way you'd treat the person you love the most in the whole wide world right now. Only with love. Now turn that same love around to you. Walk away when a situation doesn't serve you or it robs you of a moment of happiness. Not to be cliché, but life is too short for anything else. Every day matters when it could be your last. Every day I try to be true to myself. What do I want to do with my day? Whom do I want to spend it with? Who or what deserves my time on this one day without any thought about tomorrow? This was one of the hardest adjustments I made, but I found that when you're true to yourself down to, "What's for dinner" your life flows appropriately and you'll always be at ease. When you walk your own path, the universe unfolds in front of you. When you walk the path of another to take away from your own happiness, the universe throws you curve balls. It isn't easy and you feel "off." Once you feel self-love, being "off" is no longer an option.

Self-love = treating yourself how you treat your most loved one. Although it may sound selfish, putting yourself first is the most unselfish thing you can do. When I show up for myself first, everything else falls into place, including the people in my life. Things transform. People treat you differently. Happiness isn't in the distance. Instead, you realize it in the right now that everything you do in every moment counts, every time. My biggest lesson was the knowing that I'm here to be happy, not unhappy.

- Write out the most loving things you do for other people:
- Write out the most loving things you do for yourself:

MAKE SURE THEY ARE IN BALANCE!

WEEK 22: FORGIVENESS

"It's not an easy journey, to get to a place where you forgive people. But it is such a powerful place, because it frees you."

-Tyler Perry

Forgiveness has been one of the hardest places inside for me to reach on many levels. I don't know if it comes from some dark indignant place in me, or a hidden fear of looking at the actual wrong I felt, and therefore having to deal with the pain and hurt.

Forgiveness isn't a simple process. It is, however, a necessary process to keep life's possibilities flowing through you.

People hurt us all the time. Our expectations aren't met, and our life somehow unravels in the wake of other people *being people*. Sometimes it's unintentional, sometimes it's purposeful, and sometimes it's downright vengeful.

When we offer someone our forgiveness, it's because we feel we've been mistreated. When we're hurt, or someone close to us is wronged, our ability to realistically sort through the facts dissipate into thin air and we bypass what I now know to be a simple act of forgiveness.

We would rather go on to more noteworthy emotional feelings, such as self-righteousness, betrayal, revenge, resentment, rage, or anger. It's completely normal to feel these emotions when someone has wronged us. However, holding on to those emotions for years and years without forgiving that person isn't so normal.

Non-forgiveness robs you of happiness and adds to the pain you've already felt. It completely blocks the flow of good waiting to come into your life. I've found whenever I'm in a situation that requires forgiveness, I have a part, and it has always become a catalyst for great change. Sometimes it's unasked for change, but it's still change.

Without forgiveness and a true ritualistic process of letting go of our pain, we will always have "the story" inside of us. We replay it in our mind, we tell other people, we blog about it, we post passive aggressively about it, and then one day we wake up, look at it, and wonder why we wasted so much time on this issue. We ask ourselves how we allowed this person to hang around in our head for so long. Then we realize, often too late to rectify, that time will always erase the story. Yet here is where that silent lingering resentment comes up to haunt us because we "forgot" but we never forgave the person or situation, or ourselves.

Instead of starting our own internal process of forgiveness the minute we know we have been wronged, we wait for an apology, as if that will change something about the act that hurt us. Yet, unless it's a sincere apology that comes from someone's heart, it will alleviate very little.

I've spent more than enough time waiting and waiting for the apology that clearly *isn't going to come.* I've also had people "demand" apologies from me, as if somehow, forcing it from me would truly alleviate their angst. Parents teach their children to apologize all the time whether they want to or not, and then in turn they teach their children to say, "It's okay." Notice how thirty minutes later those kids are playing and laughing and enjoying life as if there's no tomorrow? It's because they forgave.

During this journey, I spent a year waiting for and expecting an apology from a few people who I believed owed me one. I've had many conversations in my head with these people, playing the scene out repeatedly *as if it was real.*

Then I realized two years had passed and there was zero chance I'd ever receive an apology, so how in the world could I ever forgive them?

My life coach suggested I write them a letter telling them everything I thought and felt about what they did, how I felt I was treated, and the consequences to my life. How hurt I was. How angry I was. How small and un-important they made me feel. The ripple effect of their actions, and their lack of compassion when they knew the truth.

Then she said, "But don't send it."

Wait. Whaaat? This was my moment! *"I want them to know all of this, and to feel how much they hurt me. I want them to agonize as they read every line. I want them to feel guilty and concerned, and miss me and claim they made a mistake. Then and only then will they be truly forgiven."*

Then I roared inside with laughter.

Hmmm, it sounded like I wanted to *hurt them*. It hit me that this lack of ability to simply offer forgiveness in the moments of pain creates a circle of un-forgiveness that's virtually impossible to escape. Round and round and round we go. I can't forgive you until you apologize, and only then if you hear all my sordid details of pain so that you hurt so much that I then *need to apologize to you.*

I was still clearly in revenge mode around this. I took on the exercise and feverishly wrote into the night. The next week when I met with my coach she asked me about the exercise and this was my actual response *"Yeah, I did it and honestly, halfway through I realized that I didn't care anymore. I realized that I was so happy it had happened because of the radical shift it caused in my life that by the end of the letter I was thanking them and further congratulating them on their own success that came from this explosion in my life. I've ironically completely lost the point of needing validation to forgive them."* I had held on to that scenario in my head for so long and in one page I was able to forgive them and let the situation leave my psyche.

It doesn't mean I like what they did. It doesn't mean it was okay. It doesn't mean we will suddenly be friends. It doesn't mean that it won't happen again to either myself or somebody else, or that I won't be triggered by similar events. It means I AM FREE from the bondage of the betrayal I felt.

Then, for a minute I felt like I was betraying myself and I realized how ridiculous that was. I'd been suffocating myself with this armor of righteousness, waiting for an apology, and now I felt guilty going on without one? It made no sense, but I want to share the whole spectrum of the forgiveness process in the hopes that this will inspire you to find forgiveness in whatever's holding you back from the beauty of this life. I want you to stop living each day harboring negative feelings because you haven't forgiven someone.

While it was clear that I had to get it out to move on, we don't always get the opportunity to forgive someone in person, and so we carry it around waiting for the day we "bump" into him or her.

The exercise freed me and freed them. They just didn't know it. In fact, they never knew it because I suspect that in their eyes they did no wrong, owed no apology, and simply did what they had to do to survive. It's that simple.

People, just being people.

When we carry the burden of what other people have "done to us," we're only hurting ourselves.

I've found there are stages to find forgiveness:

1. Acknowledge that you have been wronged, hurt, betrayed. Say it aloud to yourself. Milk it, feel it, cry about it, wear it, and then:
2. Ask yourself how you contributed to the story you're telling yourself is unforgiveable?
3. What adjectives are you adding that do not need to be there?
4. What feelings are blocking your forgiveness?
5. Tell the person(s) involved in your own way that you forgive them for being human. For me writing it out worked. For you it may be some other way. Burning a piece of paper with their names and a simple, "I forgive you." Maybe seeking professional help to get you through it. In my case, that's

what I needed to get here. Professional help is a perfect road to take if it gets you to a place of peace.

In all circumstances, have a silent conversation with this person and for the rest of your precious life, forgive and *let it go.*

My dear friend Cari Butler who teaches the Ho'oponopono Hawaiian prayer of forgiveness told me to tell myself in the simplest terms "I need to clear myself of that." Clearing yourself through forgiveness is cleaning your soul.

We're all human, and humans make mistakes. We can all preach righteousness all day long in some fashion or another, yet we're all just a small speck of light in a gigantic universe: humans, all trying to find our place in this world. I like to think we're all trying to be better somehow.

If you've ever watched a video of the universe, galaxies, and energy rolling around us, you must have considered the possibility of how small something really is, and how connected we all are. Yes, hurt feelings are hard to swallow. Pride and ego have a large voice, but so do kindness, understanding, compassion, and peace.

When I found my peace and my forgiveness, I felt like there was a light shining through me. The huge grey blob of un-forgiveness that had been hanging around for far too long was lifted from my body. I wanted to see the people I'd once loved, hug them, and let them know I understood it was just life. I may not get that moment, so I settle for distant forgiveness for them, and most importantly for myself.

At the end of every coaching session I had with my life coach, she'd ask me to take a moment and forgive myself for whatever had come up for me. Whatever I felt was honestly holding me back. I always forgave myself for all the wasted time thinking this or that thought, instead of taking action and moving on. Ultimately, I always forgave myself for being human.

I know there's darkness in the world that we cannot avoid, and that some unforgiveable acts of violence have affected each of us in a plethora of ways, but there's nothing that can't be forgiven inside of you by looking at the humanness of the act. Whenever I put myself in someone else's shoes, even if I don't agree with them, I soften.

When I say find forgiveness inside of you, it's to help you understand that this is where the action happens. Even saying "I forgive you" to someone doesn't take care of what's inside. You have to feel it emotionally. You have to try to identify the positives that came out of the situation no matter how small. Even if it meant that you took a walk because you were so angry, and as a result you saw a beautiful flower on the way. Stop and express thanks to the flower because when we find the grace and beauty in every ugly situation we encounter, no matter how small, we're brought back to the true essence of life, which is to be happy. And you cannot feel happy with grudges as it's emotionally impossible. Happiness guides you through life with your eyes wide open to possibilities, and in every single instant, possibilities arise. If you're blocked by grudges that you're holding onto, you cannot see the light in front of you.

On a replay of a Super Soul Sunday (7/29/12) Marianne Williamson author of A Return to Love said *"If you want a situation to change, pray for them."* - *"If I pray for your happiness, one of two things will happen: either you will behave differently, or I won't care."* Amen. I knew as soon as I heard it exactly what she meant.

The most impressive piece of this for me was the "I won't care." With six months to live, I have to find forgiveness for all the people who have wronged me, or for whom I've carried a long-standing resentment. When I leave this planet I'll be clean and loved and everyone in my world will know the part they played, good or bad. I'll leave with no one to forgive because of the way I now live.

This was no easy exercise. In order to get all of this out of my happy place, I really wanted to clear this piece up. I made a list of all the things, people, and circumstances I needed to forgive. Then I made a list of all the things I wanted to forgive myself for. Here are some of the more general statements I made:

I forgive you for the first punch you gave me at age fourteen, therefore shaping the way I let myself be treated for the rest of my life.

I forgive you for stealing from me.

I forgive you for talking about me in a way that hurt me.

I forgive you for putting other people ahead of me when I needed your time and love. I understand you were just doing your best.

I forgive you for leaving me when I needed you the most.

I forgive you for the choice you made where you put yourself before others and I perceived you as selfish.

I forgive you for being human.

This was the easy part, because when I started to think about forgiving the "great wrongs" I couldn't come up with a lot that I hadn't already let go.

Then came the hard part. Forgiving myself.

I forgive you for making a choice that would hurt your body and suffocate your spiritual channel.

I forgive you for moving twenty-three times when you had many opportunities to stay put and have a feeling of home.

I forgive your gypsy soul that has caused havoc in your life.

I forgive your temper and harsh reactions to simple things, and the time you slapped someone for doing you "wrong" instead of talking to them.

I forgive you for your constant worry and need to control everything.

I forgive you for pleasing everybody else before yourself to set up a lifetime of phoniness.

I forgive you for the times you just gave up.

I forgive you for not having faith.

I forgive you for making choices that didn't serve your highest good when you knew this stuff.

I forgive you for hurting other people in the process.

I forgive you for thinking you had to hide your truth instead of owning it for so long that you wasted so much authentic precious time not allowing your soul to evolve.

I forgive you for every person you have judged.

I forgive you for every person you have walked by without giving them deserved eye contact.

I forgive you for not always following your heart.

Questions to Ponder

Take a moment and ask yourself where you are holding onto a grudge in your life with someone that you have not forgiven.

Ask yourself:

- Whom do I need to forgive that I've been unable to forgive?

- How is holding onto this situation serving my life today?

- What do I need from this person to forgive them?

Now write them the letter. Let them have it. Get every sorted detail out on paper in front of you. All the hurt, what they did to your life, how it affected you, how long it has affected you for, the circumstances you believe led to the wrong. Leave nothing out as nothing is too severe to say. Say it all right here, right now.

It's my belief that when you do this you will find forgiveness for them inside.

Then forgive yourself for allowing it to go on inside you for so long. Wake up tomorrow FREE!

WEEK 23: WHAT IS DEATH...REALLY?

"Death is a stripping away of all that is not you. The secret to life is to 'die before you die' — and find that there is no death."

-Eckhart Tolle

March 5, 1999

It was hard to look back and realize that fifteen years had gone by. It could have been fifteen weeks or fifteen minutes. When a person close to your heart passes on to the next "realm" there's no such thing as time. There's no question that we miss them in a physical sense, but it amazes me that the impact of their spirit can stay here with us forever. This has to say something about "the other side."

I've always believed that a higher power life force existed outside of the human experience. Scientists agree. More and more people believe it, spiritual leaders treat it like gospel, and people like me or you who can't really put their finger on "it," somehow still know "it."

God, Spirit, Heaven is everywhere. It's in the majestic changing colors in nature. Alternatively, the butterfly who flutters by precisely when you need something to believe in. I recently watched a video on You tube that showed the changing seasons of the same landscapes throughout one year. It was miraculous to see the vision of snow and ice turn to green grass blades, flowers turn to dry bush, and sunflowers turn to the magic of the fall leaves. It was the most beautiful and simple definition of the circle of life and death. Then being reborn again.

I was fortunate enough in this human experience to know it exists. In Christmas 1998, my Mother presented me with a book written by a famous psychic called Sylvia Brown. Mom was reading the same book. We were both avid fans of her and her ability to "know" things.

Three weeks later my Mother was given her own "six months to live sentence" Unfortunately and unbeknownst to any of us it transpired to be a six-week sentence.

They had found a tumor and wanted to go in and explore. This diagnosis would explain the fainting and dizzy spells and her complaint of the summer heat that past year.

She had just retired in August, three short months before. She thought her off feeling of wellbeing was life's way of saying you've worked much harder than you should have for all the wrong reasons, and its now time to relax. She had big plans to travel, read, and write that book she'd always wanted to write. To walk more and smoke less. To be the wife she thought my Father wanted after years of being a Mother above all else.

In her eyes, she looked at it as a routine exploration. A simple in-out procedure. Her biggest fear had come true. I remember regularly hearing throughout my life that she'd only live until she was sixty-five. Her own Mother passing away at age fifty-eight from cancer conditioned her that she was going to follow the same path. Clearly her thought pattern created this reality, however I only know that now when I catch myself thinking the same dooming thoughts. After years of conditioning that it was her reality, it became mine as well.

At age forty, I was stricken with two choices. I could either let my conditioned mind make the same reality for my children and myself, or realize that I couldn't possibly "know" when I am going to "die." It was important to gain understanding and know that all I have is right this very minute. I chose to think the opposite of cancer every time the thought entered my mind.

Her mind was plotting a little radiation, a little chemotherapy and then she'd be on her way to fulfilling her dream of retirement.

I lived two hours away with three kids and a granddaughter, plus I had a full time job, and although I didn't want to be anywhere else but there, my chosen lifestyle had me traveling the roads daily to do it all. I have to say that now fifteen years later as guilty as I felt about leaving my responsibilities, I'm so grateful that I did. There's nothing more important in those 'drop everything' moments when you race to be by your loved one's side. I knew I had my life to come back to. My Mother only thought she did.

Immediately after the "exploration" surgery, they told us she wouldn't wake up and the tests indicated that the cancer had spread all over her body, lungs, liver, and kidneys. They told us she had forty-eight hours to live. "Call who you need," they said.

My Father turned pale. He had been married to my mother for forty-five years, and he realized he was losing his best friend. He said to me with the most desperate look I'd ever seen on his face, "I just need her to wake up."

The doctor left us and then suddenly, without warning, standing at the hospital room door where my brother, Father and I had been sitting a softly spoken man appeared in the doorway and said, "Courage. You'll need to have courage." Then as suddenly as he appeared, he disappeared. My brother walked the few steps to the door, and then looked both ways to empty halls. He asked the attending nurse staff if they had seen the gentleman who just walked out of the room and they all replied "no."

We all hear stories like this and wonder if they're true. I like to believe it was a soul passed to take her onto her next journey. I was unaware at that moment how much courage I'd need.

Then something miraculous happened.

Against the entire doctor's prognosis, she woke up. For five long days, she was coherent enough for the people who loved her to sadly say goodbye. I wouldn't know how loved this woman was until I witnessed the friends who came to say goodbye and the 250 people community-wide who attended her funeral.

My Mother was so much more than I'd ever known.

It was day five on Friday at 1:30 pm and everyone had gone. It had become too difficult for the rest of our family to watch as her body functions began to shut down. If you've ever witnessed a person dying from cancer you know that it's in several stages and at the end, there's a toxic shutdown. My father said his final goodbye, and told me he wouldn't be coming back.

I looked at my brother and asked him, "What are you doing this weekend?" "Nothing," he said. I had no plans either so I took a shot. "What do you say we stay with her for the rest of the weekend so she doesn't have to be alone?" I couldn't stand the thought of leaving her alone to die, no matter how hard it was to watch her body deteriorate. We had only known the news for five days. My own spirit was in a great deal of turmoil. He agreed, and we decided to go and get a bite to eat. That lunch goes down in my history book as the most important meal of my life, as we connected so honestly in a way I'll always remember.

It was a moment I know neither of us will forget. During that lunch, I formed the belief that the dying give us far more gifts of joy then we are able to credit in the moment of death, and a basic realization of how precious life is. Death teaches us how important people are, and how unimportant "stuff" is.

Back upstairs, I was on one side of the bed, he was on the other, at the foot of the bed, each of us taking turns to stroke her, feed her ice chips, and whisper in her ear that it was ok to let go. We pleaded for her to "go to the light." It was all I knew to do. It took tremendous courage to let her go.

She was a fighter, and she clearly didn't want to leave us. We could see her spirit fighting to stay, to complete her dreams of retirement.

An hour or two went by and I began to read my psychic book. I got to chapter eight – a meditation called THE LABROTORY. The goal of this meditation was to heal yourself or other people by putting them/you on a table surrounding yourself/them with light and using a powerful healing energy sucking the pain, physical or emotional problem right out of them. I thought to myself, "Why wouldn't this work to help my Mother with her struggle to let go?"

I began the meditation by putting my mother on the table and picturing angels all around her. In an instant, my third eye woke up. I saw my Mother's face at the end of the table, but her body was now a flowing white mass of what looked like angels; long strands of white gauze flowing in the air around what was once her physical body. It was scary and very unknown territory, but for some reason, fear was not winning.

I suddenly saw her rising off the table in the most beautiful way you could imagine. Light was everywhere and the angels were flowing in a space-like field. The only thing I could now see was the spirit. With my eyes still shut, I said to my brother, "She's letting go." I opened my eyes to look at her and she took three deep cleansing breaths and was gone. Peacefulness filled the room.

I was lifted out of my chair. I don't remember standing up, and my brother and I on each side of her, held hands and looked up for a while, drenched in her spirit that now surrounded the room. It was abundantly clear that her spirit had lifted and left, and that the body we had watched for days deteriorate before our eyes was just that – a body, a shell that was housing her spirit. In that moment it was forever undeniable that we never die. We only change form.

We left the hospital within minutes. I'd always felt odd about that, but the truth was she simply wasn't there anymore. I got in my car and drove straight to my parent's home to tell my Father. However, I, the non-drinker, walked straight to my Mother's liquor cabinet and poured a vodka grape (my Mother's nightly drink), and I chugged it down.

I walked into the backyard and broke the news to my Father and my three other brothers. Everyone was sad and crying and I was embarrassingly elated. I was walking on a cloud. The only way I could describe it was as if I was three feet off the ground. I almost felt guilty for feeling so good. I'd just experienced something I believe only a select few are gifted with.

I have never been afraid of death since.

Moments later, the light that my Father would never fix for my Mother turned on all on its own and shined brighter than it ever had. This simple electrical mishap gave my Father more comfort than any person could. He knew my Mother had come home.

Hours later, I was up in my Mother's room and I reached into her bedside table and saw her own copy of the psychic book and it was folded with a bookmark - on chapter eight!

Three weeks later a box of cassette tapes arrived in her name. It was a taped recording of a show that the psychic had done on a local radio station in regards to life after death. My Mother, fascinated with the subject, had ordered them before the diagnosis.

I turned on the tapes. What I heard couldn't have described any clearer for me what happens after we die. She stated that the spirit world operates on a different frequency, about three feet off the ground. I knew I'd felt that very indescribable feeling.

That night after I listened to the tapes and I was sleeping in the bed I grew up in, my Mother came to me and woke me up. It was a pulling sensation at my feet, and I felt instant fear. It scared the bejebbees out of me. I know now it was the prelude to an out of body experience.

I stood up out of bed, heart racing, fearful, and then I felt my Mother's arms tightly hug me. It wasn't a dream, I knew unequivocally that she was there and I can feel that hug as real today as I did that night.

There's no doubt in my mind that we do not "die" when we die. I forget that a lot when I stress about life. However, it was on this day, March 5, 1999 that I was able to see it in action. The only thing I ever asked my mom for when we had to face the fact that she may not survive the cancer was to show me proof that life existed on the other side "Move my mountain," I said. "Send roses or feathers flying through the sky."

What I got was far better than I could have asked for. I received actual proof that our spirit is stronger than any illness. When our physical body deteriorates and dies, our spirit takes off and soars. We miss the people who leave us in this unbearable physical sense. To know inside that the spirit lives on forever was the greatest gift my Mother could have given me besides my life.

I know our paths will cross again and I know that she is with me.

If our spirit is this strong in death, look what you can do with your spirit in life. Letting your spirit shine starts by being true to your spirit, that little knowing voice inside your heart that signals when you are in accordance with your truth. When you truly start living, you know it. When you start to "en-joy" in life, you know it.

How do we start living this way? How do we live as if each day matters?

It starts by letting go of all the things that truly do not serve you. Live your life without guilt. Keep true to your deepest values and your deepest aspirations. Take as long as it takes to learn to love yourself and pursue your dreams. It's easy to say it and up until now I had no idea how I'd accomplish this task, yet I learned that when you feel inside that you are the most important person to you on the planet – life happens.

Smile, laugh, pray, seek calmness, and seek peace. Strive for balance. Read. Play. Sing. Dance. Walk on the beach. Most importantly, breathe very deeply many times a day.

If you resonated with anything that I wrote here in my sometimes simple, sometimes complicated six month journey that I've shared with you, ***know this***: every single day of our life in an instant we and the people we cherish can be gone.

Do not wait for a death sentence to start living.

A car accident can take a life in five seconds.

A plane can explode and fall out of the sky in less than five seconds yet most of us board them with gleeful anticipation of going somewhere different, or simply back to the comfort of our own home.

People accidently fall off cliffs, out of windows, or collapse during their daily run.

You can be at work and an airplane full of terrorists can fly into your building – twice within ten minutes.

An earthquake can rumble up from the earth's core without warning and cause major catastrophes.

A tornado or a fire can whip through your community and take many lives in random sequence.

A sudden unexpected flu can take you out in five days.

You can be at a tourist attraction or in a movie theatre and be in the line of gunfire brought on by a crazy mind.

You can also die a little bit each day by living an unfulfilled life filled with angst and strife.

The simple undeniable fact of life is that we do not know when our time to die is.

I lived many years of my life in fear of this event as if I knew exactly when the moment would occur. I said no to opportunities and yes to playing it safe. I tried to eat better, exercise more, stress less, and trust more.

I tried tuning in to every God, spiritual practice, and guru on the planet, yet I was still living an unfulfilled life because I felt so afraid of death. I was afraid of change. I was afraid I'd lose somebody I loved. I worried constantly about every little thing that could potentially happen. I was afraid of living my life in the spirit life is intended to be lived. In retrospect, I was one of the zombies. I wasn't perceptive enough to understand that life could slip by me while I worried it away. I was afraid to come outside and play with the world, strangled with fear of the unknown future.

I learned to: Not take chances. Keep your head down. Keep your nose to the grindstone. Save your money. Do not trust this. Do not trust that.

I now believe that in order to live a fulfilled life, you must first stare mortality in the face. I know and you know that someday we're all going to die. I know that people I love in my everyday are going to die and there isn't anything I can do to change that.

The reality is, the next moment is the only valuable tangible asset you have. No one in the history of man has yet to solve the mystery of time. We're out here orbiting in an unknown existence that we rigidly abide by with a calendar or a clock. The television and our smart phones remind us exactly how much time has passed and how much time we have left in our day. It records with precision the time someone tried to call you, and will record when you can call them back. How long you have been "clocked" in at work. When you get to go home. Most of the time our bodies are wired to live by a clock we have created for it. Whether it's tired, or awake, healthy or sick, we put it on a schedule that we have the sole power to create!

The question is simple and provocative: What would you do differently if you knew you were going die in six months from today? What if your clock was ticking, you stopped the madness, and you lived every day as if it were your last; *as if it mattered*?

I now truly live as if each day matters, because it does.

Answering this single question changed my life. It's my hope that if you, too, are living an unfulfilled life that it will inspire you to change yours.

Life is amazing. And then it's awful. And then it's amazing again. And in between the amazing and the awful it's ordinary and mundane and routine. Breathe in the amazing, hold on through the awful, and relax and exhale during the ordinary. That's just living heartbreaking, soul-healing, amazing, awful, ordinary life. And it's breathtakingly beautiful.

-L.R. Knost

WEEK 24: SIMPLE TRUTHS ALONG THE WAY

Through this journey I found what I call truths about life through my favorite quotes and endless days of studying life and death. In closing, I want to share some of my favorite truths from websites and social media, and my thoughts about them. While writing this book almost daily I'd jot down many words of wisdom on anything from a napkin to my hand. Below is my interpretation of the truths of life that I discovered along the way:

- **"Your beliefs don't make you a better person, your behavior does**." Written on a chalkboard in front of a quaint café in Beverly Hills. This inspired me to fully start "walking my talk," and practicing what I preach.
- **"Give people high fives just for getting out of bed. Being a person is hard sometimes."** I ran across this picture on Pinterest by "Kid President." Kid President is a website that was born of the simple belief that kids have a voice. I know that on some of the hardest days of my life I still had to get out of bed, cook the children breakfast, and try to wear a smile for them. I often tried to disguise the angst or worry I was feeling with only 50 percent success. Nevertheless, I got out of bed. To live fully, you have to show up fully. Being present will help dissipate those feelings of despair, and to be present for your children is the greatest gift you can give them.
- **"Had I not created my whole world, I certainly would have died in other people's."** This quote by Anais Nin,

a famous French novelist, tells us as simply as possible that we cannot live someone else's life. Many times I've forsaken my own preferences, needs, and desires for another to have theirs, thinking this was the most loving way I could be. I've learned how to create my own world through self-love, and as a result other people are living theirs. It turns out they're perfectly capable of living their own lives without my help. What a concept!

- **"Your true happiness happens when you discover that no one other than yourself is responsible for the way you feel." Abraham Hicks** I now find it to be that simple, *if* you stay true to your feelings. It took me months to distinguish what my true feelings were as I climbed out of the fog of my life, but this quote reminded me that I always had a choice in how I felt. How I responded and which way a situation went solely depended on me. I can't stress how freeing this one thought is. You are the only person who knows what is truly right for you, and you're responsible for keeping yourself in alignment with that. I know life is much too short for anything else.

- **"Don't live the same year seventy-five times and call it a life." Robin Sharma** It's always hard to step out of the patterns we create, but if you aren't happy, you can stop living that way. I'm acutely aware now that evolving, learning, trying new things, and branching out of our comfort zone fully embraces this ride called life. If we keep repeating the same things over and over, we will stagnate. We won't grow and it won't be very fun. I used to like to play it safe and keep things the same, afraid to reach into the great unknown. I know now that to truly live a blissful life while I'm graced with the time to be here, I want it to be joyous and easy. I also want it to be different enough each day to challenge and delight me.

- **"Don't quit your daydream." unknown author**. Nothing has been more exciting than to find a passion and go for it. At the beginning of this journey, I had no idea what my passion or calling in life was, and I agonized about this truth on a daily basis. Striving not to be hooked into television because I had no job to go to, I spent a lot of time in silence. This allowed for a lot of daydreaming. The funny thing is by concentrating on my daydreams, they became a reality. Our busy daily lives seldom allow time for a moment of life that can validate or clarify our dreams. We have to take the time. I'd meditate in the mornings to find my inner truth and then I'd take one step, no matter how small, towards the big dream. I found my calling in the silence.

- **"Don't worry, it's just five minutes," he said**. "Five minutes?" she responded. "Five minutes is everything! Hell, one minute is everything when you're staring at your life." I paused the television when I heard this line on an episode of Chasing Life. This is probably the simplest truth I've ever heard. The character had been diagnosed with a fatal disease and was reeling with thoughts of everything she had known to be safe being ripped from her. She was grasping for some kind of control in a situation where she now had none and she suddenly became extremely clear on what was important. I paused because it made me think. Have you ever been going on in your daily life thinking everything is going just as planned, and then the phone rings and your life is suddenly changed forever? Life is so unpredictable that every minute really does matter. I never worried about how much time I had left, but what if we lived our life moment to moment with a "back of your mind knowing" that every minute does count. If we truly started living this way, we'd appreciate every moment. A mere second can change our life forever.

- **"You can't be both awesome and negative. Choose one." Karen Salmansohn**. Again, a quote from Pinterest. Karen's website notsalmon.com reads, "Self-help for people who wouldn't be caught dead doing self-help." I loved this! Anybody can grasp this concept. It's so simple to understand that in order to be awesome, feel awesome, and do awesome stuff in this life, we can't be negative. Negative thoughts are so strong. Watch the momentum of negative thoughts get the ball rolling. I've studied, read, and heard for decades about the power of thought, absorbing every drop of information I could on how we can create our entire lives with our thoughts. We have to remember it is us and us alone that keep the drama going. You can turn it around by not feeding your negative thoughts. If you've ever taken a moment with a negative thought, you know what I'm talking about. I usually don't allow them anymore, but I'm human. So just for the sake of knowing this one simple truth, allow a negative thought, watch how it grows, and feeds one after the other until there's absolutely no room for anything else to come in. It's so toxic. Now think an awesome thought; a feel giddy, scrumptious, loving, and able to guide you effortlessly through your life thought. Now choose one to keep. I rest my case.

- **"Under think it." Author unknown.** How many times have you "over thought" something and created a made-up scenario that you were sure was the truth? Until you found out it wasn't. I now choose to let life happen every day without my muddled, stressful thoughts messing it all up. The Universe knows what's up and what your desired life is at all times. All you have to do is trust yourself enough to walk right into it in divine timing. My dear friend & motivational speaker Rakale Hannah, author of the forthcoming book How to Give An Apology like a Pro, says, "There are no mistakes." Therefore, I say there's no reason to over think anything. One day you'll wake up and discover that nothing was random or in error. It all unfolded exactly as it was supposed to. I'm living proof.

- **"You weren't born to just work, pay bills, and die."** **Sun-gazing.com** This is my personal favorite. We were born to enjoy life, learn about life, and be happy. I lost count of how many people told me that if faced with a "six months to live" sentence the first thing they would do is quit their job. Then pay all their debt so they didn't leave it behind. It saddened me to think that so many of us stay in our jobs to pay the bills that we incur through massive credit card debt we create, trying to be happy. Twice now, I have consolidated credit card debt by adding it to my mortgage as if that held the key to paying it off. As a result, my savings will have to pay my debt if I die before it's paid. Sorry kids but I won't spend my life working to pay bills, nor do I want this to be your truth. I've learned that financially, if you allow it, abundance has a resilient way of finding you. You just have to trust the process. I've never, even when I lost everything, not been able to count on a serendipitous event to miraculously follow and take care of my financial fear. This one truth allows me to enjoy my life in a balanced way. Sure, I have to work. I definitely have to pay bills and I try to generate income every single day. I don't, however, allow myself to worry about it and I rely on the unlimited universal financial protection to carry me through. I never let my mind wander back to the work, pay bills, sleep lifestyle. I trust that money will come my way every time I need it. I've seen it happen too many times to think any differently. shrem brezee (google it)

- **"When all else fails, take a vacation." Betty Williams** Vacation is the food for the soul. Don't turn down any opportunity to go on vacation. It's the very thing you need to keep feeling joyful in a mostly busy life. I've been accused of taking too many vacations recently, and I just nod and acknowledge with glee; "Yes, I do take a lot of vacations," and then I let them ponder it. Some people, oddly, even resent it.

- **"Life is one long apology." Marlyn L. Rice** I've learned to apologize when I'm wrong, and I've learned to not apologize for being who I am. It's that simple. The minute you apologize for who you are, you're no longer standing in alignment of your truth. The minute you step away from who you are, all bets are off.

- **"Life is 10 percent what happens to us and 90 percent how we react to it." Dennis P. Kimbro** If I can change one thing about me it'll be to learn how to respond instead of reacting. Imagine the freedom.

- **"No matter how dark, spirit always sends the light." Mastin Kipp** I now try to always look up. When things happen that we can't control that send us spiraling down to the ground, look up! Get off the floor and know that it's always darkest near the dawn, and that light will always be there. When you know this on a deep level, you can get through anything.

- **"Sit or stand but don't wobble." Dan Millman** Have to make a tough decision? Wobbling is the worst thing you can do. Making choices and jumping into a new way of living is not easy, but it's far worse to be stuck on the fence wondering which side to jump to. Make a decision, trust the universe has your back, and go towards it fearlessly.

- **"Nothing is permanent in this wicked world, not even our troubles." Charlie Chaplin** Such helpful advice. Often when we think we cannot go on, we remember that this too shall pass. Nothing stays the same. Wounds heal, hearts mend, people forgive, and life goes on.

- **"Slow is the new fast. Make the moment last."** I bought a picture of a turtle painted in the messy artist sort of way from a vendor at Venice Beach. I hang it over my desk in my office to remind me of the fatal disease I just cured myself of, called MULTI-TASKING! This is the deadliest of them all! Do one thing and you'll do it great. Do ten things at once and nothing will get done. I leave this journey banishing multi-tasking from my life forever!

- **"Mind your own business"** This simple phrase will make your life so much happier! Many news stations around the country make some of the most personal disclosures about celebrities and athletes that honestly, I sometimes cringe at the level of invasiveness that goes on. I don't need to know your business. You don't need to know mine.

- **"Everything happens for a reason"** Hands down, the most important thing to remember when things you have no control of begin rolling into your life. Know this simple truth and you will ride through the most challenging times with grace. I am living proof of this simple truth.

I will leave you with possibly my favorite movie quote on this subject:
In the words of Andy Dufresne from the Shawshank
Redemption – "Get busy living or get busy dying"

CHANGES IN ME:

Most days I allow my inner clock to wake me up. Slowly. I don't usually watch the morning news unless it's happy or world changing.

I dream BIG. I allow every outlandish dream to go on the list of things I want to be, do or have in this lifetime. I constantly refill the bucket list. I think about them, plot them on paper, and try to take an action step no matter how small towards fulfilling those dreams.

I say yes to almost every fun thing that comes my way because I appreciate what every experience can bring me.

I say no when I want to say no. This is huge because before I was a 'yes to everybody' girl. Saying no still doesn't happen often to the people I love, but the difference is they know it's a possible answer now, and somehow that gained me respect I hadn't felt before.

I don't tolerate unnecessary drama in my life. Period.

I give no explanations for why I do something, want to do something, or have just done something.

I say I love you a lot more to those I love. I hear it a lot more too. I notice when my children say it, which through the process I noticed is every time we part!

I hug more. I gift more. I thank people more. I appreciate what people do for me. I let them know.

I take a moment when I'm wrong to look people in the eyes with my truth to make sure they hear me when I say I'm sorry or I want to clarify.

When other people are wrong, I pull up my big girl pants and I let them know. This is a hard one, but it is important to stand up for what you know is true for you.

I find time for people when they ask. I advise when they ask. I help them sort through their stuff without judgment. I try to make them laugh. I love that they ask instead of feeling as if it is an inconvenience, and that taught me a lot about myself.

I don't worry about money. I know I can't take it with me, and I know I'll always have enough no matter what the circumstances. Therefore, I'm generous and I share anything I can. I can't hold onto to or hoard anything at all anymore. I spend with the perception that I'm helping somebody by spending, and therefore more is going to come back to me. It is just money, or actually paper. A simple energy exchange.

I meditate daily (ok, so four to five days a week). I always find my peace when I do. It helps me check in with my inner self in a way I never knew possible. It quiets the voices (the little voices that act out those insane, usually far-fetched scenes we create).

I'm interested in just about everything now. I can't get enough information about history, why we are here, and what the big life answers are. Therefore, I read a lot.

I connect. I reach out when my inner voice says reach out. I call instead of text when I can. I want to hear a voice. Certain people come into my thoughts; I used to believe thinking about them was enough, but now I let them know.

I make dates, even if it's a year in advance, to visit the people I love who live far away.

I smile at strangers every day. I know everyone is fighting his or her own battle. I also know that every encounter matters, no matter how big or small. I know it's all part of a very intricate plan. A smile can literally change somebody's day. I no longer believe in random, unless its random acts of kindness, which I believe I could spend my entire life doing and be in complete bliss. I've learned there's no warmer feeling inside then making a difference in somebody else's life, and so I hope this book will make a difference in your life and in the lives of all the people around you!

I can hear Dr. Wayne Dyer's words "none of us are getting out of here alive" ring in my ear daily. I want to live each day mattering to someone. There is a global movement across the world where people are waking up to the awareness that there is so much more to life then strife. If you enjoyed this book, share it with someone who needs it. Share it on Social Media. Make each day count in your world. Be confident every day that when you leave this existence, you have *made* a difference. That is what I believe life, is all about.

"How to be at peace now? By making peace with the present moment. The present moment is the field on which the game of life happens. It cannot happen anywhere else"

-Eckhart Tolle

THANK YOU!

I understand fully why every actor initially thanks GOD when they win the Oscar. Without the universal inspirational voice and force of spirit, this book would not have happened. I am so grateful for the ability to listen to my inner voice and spirits guiding words who have a place on each page of this book. On a human level, I would like to thank the following people for their part in my life and this book.

Keidi Keating - The Book Angel. I took a shot and reached out to you through a twitter post (ironically) and you knocked my socks off with your editing. I cannot thank you enough for turning this book into something everyone can understand. Your words of encouragement were just what I needed to hear at a moment I wanted to shelve it. THANK YOU! You are the best!

Balboa Press- Maneli Reihani, Virginia Morrel and Rebecca Hogue. Thank you, thank you, thank you. Working with all of you was a great joy. Thank you for your patience, flexibility and Rebecca for your kindred spirit! Its no mystery you were the one to call and dig my story out of me. On to the next book!

Kimberly Nigro, Leah M. Anderson Mendoza, Florence Moorhead-Rosenburg, Debra Spiliotis, and Tony Bosque. Thank you from the bottom of my heart for sharing your personal stories and inspiring people to live a better life through your experiences. Your dedication and support for my need to share a message with the world made this a better book. Eternally yours.

Nancy Levin- I often shudder to think what my world would have been like the last two years without you in it. You are an amazing Author, Poet, Life Coach, Mentor and Friend. Through you I found me. Through your groups I have made friends I cannot live without. I am so, so very grateful for you in my life. I am so grateful for the excavation you led me through to become who I am. You pushed me when I needed to be pushed, and you pulled me when I couldn't get there. You gave me the confidence and self-worth to "go for it" -Thank you from every cell in my body. I love you.

Rakale Hannah- Without your tenacious spirit in my life this book and my website would definitely have sat 98% done for who knows how much longer. You are the reason I kept going. You were a cheerleader when I needed it, and a boss when I needed it. Watching you grow and soar with your own projects while making sure I was growing with you, was so inspirational. So much grattitude for you. Thank you my friend. You are forever etched in my heart.

Dorena Kohrs – You are such a sweet surprise in my life, no matter how far away from me your are! When I was in the midst of negative feedback you gave me such affirmation that I was on to something, to keep going and when to be done. You took time out of your busy life to read, comment and validate my words. (and you had to read the draft yikes!) Thank you for being my friend and for the push to keep going.

Denise Nelson - We have never met in person which makes this friendship we have built mean so much to me. You took time to help me through some uncomfortable stuff and process many areas of life to gain more clarity. You are an amazing life coach and friend, and I am so grateful for you and our morning talks.

Nina Kirby and **Kim Egide Reppucci** – My cheerleaders, my support and my sounding boards = Unconditional Friendship. Thank you for always rallying around me through all the ups and downs of my life and for the adventures having you in my life has brought. I cannot imagine a life without you in it. (**Bri Kirby, Angie Kirby & "Tal" Kirby** – ditto)

To all my Worthy/Jump sisters - you have had such an undeniable impact on this journey and transformation with me, particularly - **Barbara Rudzki Ridener**- **Lisa Rock, Denise Nelson, Denise Stricklin Ackerman, Julie Jacky, Kathleen Mullaney Powers, Laura Pavelka Wright, Mindy Fisher, Liz Miller Klein, Lisa Eidenberg, Julie Stroud, Mary C. Coleman, Lidia Beutner, Dana Leisegang, Monika Kovacs, Laura Fox, Sarah Grace, Susan Myhr Fritz, Amy Hood Kazer, Chara Rodriguera, Christine Corbett Gipple, Elizabeth Campbell, Holly Asmus Tharaldson, Jessica Valor, Karen Fitzgerald, Kim Julen, Paula Marchetti Kaufman, Found Me -Heather, Dorena Kohrs,Rakale Hannah; I LOVE YOU.** How we grew together was life changing. Can we get a collective shout out to Nancy Levin for bringing us together! I am humbled and awed by your spirits and your amazing accomplishments. To all my readers: **Google these names!** These women are out here changing the world in ways you cannot imagine!

Cari Butler- You entered my life in the most serendipitous way I have ever experienced. We met face to face for the first time in line at the bathroom. It goes down in my history book as the most memorable connection I have ever made. What amazed me was that we have practically talked every day since we met – as if we had known each other our entire lives. I suppose we have. Thank you for giving me actual proof that spirit and Angels exist.

Special shout out to **Carol Ann Weber, Rebecca Jackson from Higher Love, Dr. Niama Williams,** & a double thanks to **Chara Rodriguera** and **Rakale Hannah**-. I am so grateful for our connection.

Carmen King- Thank you for being my friend in addition to being an amazing photographer. (Loved the pics)

Michael Holmes – You are the definition of "friends who will ride in the bus with you when the limo breaks down" One phone call to you and you rocked my world with your unconditional friendship, your savvy lawyer skills and your genuine concern that I would be okay. Thank you from the bottom of my heart. I owe you and I will never forget that!

Staci Webster- You lived a lot of this life with me and you will always be my "best friend". You asked me a million times "when do I get to read the book"? When you finally got it- *You didn't have time.* It caused me to pause and look again at why I was even writing this book- and I realized it was precisely for people just like us who think they *do not have time* to stop and change their lives. We have been great mirrors for each other. Thank you for always being there for me, I am grateful for all the opportunities our friendship has created.

Sweet Melissa Cash and Zorah Pearl Everson- You are so deep in my heart. I will never forget that "one summer" of bonding like no other. All we had was each other and I am so grateful for having you both during that time in my life and for the the memories we shared. Love you both forever and ever.

Traci Farmer Elmore, Franke Christensen, Tammy Jones, Tonia Payne and Nadine Delapo– My ride or die BFF's- Original OG's & BGC's- Thank you for being my friends, I never would have made it in this town without you.

Sandy Peters and my friends from the classroom at ROP – You rallied and helped me graduate from high school during this journey which was no easy fete at my age. Thank you for your friendship and Sandy, for being the amazing teacher that you are.

Dr. B – otherwise known as **Brad Kammer** – Mind - Body therapist. I cannot thank you enough for sitting through hours and hours of "my story" and for helping me find my worth. I hope you will enjoy this book, as you more than anyone know every part of my plight.

To my RHC family- Cameron Johnson- you're the best boss I could ever ask for. Thank you for holding me together with some semblance of a job when I had none. To my water **girls Mary Bell, Sue Murphy, Clarissa Koehn, Susy Hardy, Kayla Meadows, Flo Passof, Sharon Grover, Jane Berry, Suzy Byrd, Lori & Bee Martinez**–My "wake up" crowd. You are the *only* reason I will get up at 5 am twice a week- period. Thank you for being there for me during some of the roughest days of my life.

Kevin Britton, Nikki Burgess, Estelle Clifton, Teresa Baarts, Jennifer Bartolomei,Marrissa Jones, Lisa Marie Williams, Brant Brooks- Miss you guys to the moon. Thank you for your support and heartfelt concern as you watched me break. As Brant said to me at the end *" It was a good run"* Your unconditional friendship etched on my heart.

Robin Johnson, Jo Nigro, Cam Leith, Cate Cooper – barely a post went by on my Facebook page that you all didn't "like" or comment on. I cannot tell you how that helped me stay focused on my path to finish this book. It means the world to me that you supported me and that I was able to inspire you. I've always said, at the end of the day, 'If I inspire just one…..it is worth it" Thank you so much.

Miss Nikki Minaj, Rhianna & Kelly Clarkson - your music got me through some of the hardest moments – "Fly" – and "What doesn't kill you - makes you stronger" were my theme songs during this journey. I'm quite sure if they ever come up at a Kareoke bar, I will win ! (yes I know every note)

Mastin Kipp- The day I 'won" the "Night with Mastin" in San Francisco so randomly during this journey was life changing. You taught me how to breathe in Kundalini yoga which allowed me to dig deeper inside than I ever had and see a moment of clarity that changed everything - in every relationship, IT TAKES TWO. A twitter post changed your life – mine too Thank you.

Laura Cook, Mel Hyman, Anita and the entire staff at UCSF Children's Hospital. You will always be in my heart. Thank you for saving my daughter's life.

To Megan, Austin and Jarrett- my children- You have put up with a lot having me as your mom. Thank you for your unconditional love and support throughout my life and some of the life changing choices I made that you had to reap. You are the reason I got up every morning when I didn't think life was very fair. Through your lives (and your wives) I was able to feel a love I never knew existed through your own children. "Love you."

To my Grandchildren -Chantial, Calogero, Abriana and Jahselle- My joy! Thank you for picking us to grow with. I hope to not let you down. My heart grew bigger with each one of you.

To Erika Anello and Yazmin Buenrostro- Thank you for giving me the greatest joy/gifts I have ever felt through my grandchildren. You are amazing Mothers and I am so grateful for you both.

To my Anello Family: Rob, Barry, Maia, Tony, Sue, Anthony, Dino, Kristy, Sophia, Jake, Ryan Paul and Vinny- you are my everything. To my favorite people on the planet – Jules Anello & Matt Evans, (thank you for allowing me to share your story and sharing your own thoughts with me about life and what it is like to look at the potenial end of it) My dear **Cousin Donna Labagh & family**- So happy you are in my life, and we are able to bond as a family- your love for my grandmother will never be forgotten! You are all my peeps. My Tribe. I am so grateful to have your love & your friendship, share your highs, your lows and understanding that we are in this together. We are the definition of family. Thank you.

To Tulua Vea (CiCi) and Lavinia Vea (Nia) – Thank you for taking such good care of my gram. You two are truly angels on earth.

Special thanks to my brother Dino- Thank you for your push, your ideas, your proof that nothing is random and your fighting -always win- no matter what spirit! Not to mention your great writing. It's our year – We always wanted to be famous (wink wink)

To my BF- Brad Meier- When I lost my job and the life we knew together crumbled, you told me to find my passion. Here it is. Thank you for your support through the writing of this project. I know it took away from many days and nights we would have had. We have been through so much together- thank you for the love, the challenges, and the tenacity to see this through. KNO!

To my Grandmother Carmel Derenzo Anello age 105- Thank you for being there for me throughout your entire life. You were the one constant I could always depend on. I love you more than words could describe. Thank you for showing me what a full life means.

Last but not least- Thank You Mom and Thank You Dad. Thank you for giving me my life.

Shout out to Facebook

Not sure exactly how I would have survived without Facebook and the role it played in my connections with humans when I wanted to shut out the world. It was a huge part of my recovery. By reaching out to the masses of people I was able to discern what they really felt was important, and what really mattered in the big scheme of things. I asked the question:

What would you do if you knew you only had six months to live?

It didn't surprise me that most everyone who responded said they would savor every moment with their family and friends, and speak the words we sometimes don't take the time to speak. Most everyone declared that with this knowledge they would spend every moment they could with their loved ones, and plan huge parties to celebrate their lives together. They would go ahead and quit their dead end jobs and seek out what makes them feel most alive. They would seek out joy and passion in everyday they had left. They wanted to hug longer. Laugh more. Spend more time with family. Take more risks, and not let fear rule their choices. Eat what they wanted to eat. Go where they wanted to go. Most importantly, let things go that really did not matter.

I struggle to think we only live this way when we are faced with our mortality and it is my hope that by reading and resonating with any part of this book, you too will make the changes to live as if each day mattered.

***ASK YOURSELF** – If I only had six months to live – what would now be most important.....and then, begin to live each day "fearlessly" as if it was your last.*

My Inspiration

Reading is a favorite past-time of mine and I wanted to share here some of the books that had a great impact on my journey to live life every day as if.........(the funnest part is the research).

Conversations with God book 1,2,3 – Neale Donald Walsch

The Power of Now – Eckhart Tolle

The Four Agreements – don Miguel Ruiz

Jump...and your life will appear- an inch-by-inch guide to making a major change- Nancy Levin

(want a change? Read this book, join her groups – I promise you and your life will never be the same) www.nancylevin.com/free

The 5 Top Regrets of the Dying – Bronnie Ware

The After-life of Billy Fingers – Annie Kagan

The Ultimate Happiness Prescription – Deepok Chopra

Dying To Be Me – Anita Moorjani

The Top Ten Things Dead People Want you to Know – Mike Dooley

The Right Questions – Debbie Ford

21 Days to Master Inner Peace – Dr. Wayne Dyer

Change your thoughts- Change your life -Dr. Wayne Dyer

The Happiness Project – Gretchen Rubin

The Tethered Soul- Michael Singer (probably my favorite book of all time)

Simple Reminders – Bryant McGill

Goddesses Never Age – Christiane Northrup

May Cause Miracles – Gabby Bernstein

I'd Change my Life if I had more Time – Doreen Virtue PhD.

I Knew Their Hearts: Jeff Olsen with Lee Nelson

Evidence of Eternity – Mark Anthony

Until I say Goodbye-Susan Spencer- Wendel

E2- Pam Grout

Law of Attraction – Jerry and Esther Hicks

Ask and it is Given – Jerry & Esther Hicks

You Can Heal your Body – Louise Hay

Second Firsts- Live, Laugh and Love again – Christina Rasmussen

ABOUT THE AUTHOR

Catherine Anello is a Certified Angel Card Intuitive, Author, Fitness Instructor, Mentor and inspiration to all who know her. Her passion for spirituality and emotional health evolved into a two decade long part-time stint as an aerobics instructor, leading classes and motivating people to strengthen their bodies through movement, their mind with humor and their spirit through thought provoking questions asked at the end of each class.

Her last "real" job that lasted 12 years, averaged 50 hours of work each week in a highly stressful toxic work environment, and it left her in a constant state of stress and anxiety. One twitter post proclaiming life had to change led to a journey of inner questions on how to live a more fulfilled life. When she suddenly lost her job, she unsuspectingly suffered from PTSD in its wake. This inspired her to spend the next year shunning her chosen career in lieu of finding her true self and gaining the inner strength to allow her to live a better life.

Shedding all of the normal conditioned ways of life, Cathy allowed her seeking spirit to guide her into a "new" way of life. By tackling the little things that she never had time to experience - she noticed a strange feeling – ALIVENESS. An unavoidable passion for living life to its fullest. This sense of no obligation permitted her to stop living a future life in her mind and discover the true meaning of living for today.

Cathy is the Author of "cathslife" www.cathslife.com, a weekly blog on self-love, family love & global love issues we all face, and for her "side hustle" she runs a tax preparation office part time in the tax season. You can find Cathy Anello on Facebook; on Twitter @ cathslife, Instagram @cathslife or her Facebook Author page - Cathy Anello– Six Months to Live – Making Each Day Matter - where she inspires her followers with life quotes and shares challenging life experiences geared to validate what her followers are hungry for: being happy every day.

Contact Cathy on her website www.cathyanello.com

63600930R00131

Made in the USA
Lexington, KY
11 May 2017